Garden Color
Annuals & Perennials

By the Editors of Sunset Books and Sunset Magazine

Lane Publishing Co., Menlo Park, California

Acknowledgments

We'd like to express our appreciation to the homeowners who allowed us to photograph their gardens. And for their expert help in preparing this book, we say a special thank-you to the following people and organizations: Ed Carman, Nurseryman; Filoli Center; Nancy Clarke Hewitt; Molbak's Greenhouse & Nursery; Western Hills Rare Plant Nursery.

Supervising Editor
John K. McClements

Research & Text
Philip Edinger

Staff Editors
Kathryn L. Arthurs
Susan Warton

Design
Sandra Popovich

Illustrations
Susan Jaekel
Sandra Popovich

Photographers

All photographs in this book were taken by **Ells Marugg** with the following exceptions:

William Aplin: 21 left. **Robert Bander:** 50 bottom left. **Glenn M. Christiansen:** 27 top left. **Jerry Fredrick:** 33 bottom right, 37 bottom right, 59 top right. **Tad Goodale:** 25, 38 bottom left. **Margaret McKinnon:** 21 bottom right. **Steve W. Marley:** 57 bottom right, 59 bottom right. **Allan Mitchell:** 35 bottom right. **Don Normark:** 34 bottom, 37 top right. **Norman A. Plate:** 33 left, 39, 55 top right. **Bill Ross:** 20 bottom, 32, 53, top right, 57 bottom left. **Darrow M. Watt:** 19 top left.

Cover: Kaleidoscope of annuals and perennials combines sweet alyssum, zinnias, geraniums, gloriosa daisies, marguerites, and perennial asters. Marigolds, in the front, are in pots. Photographed by Ells Marugg. Cover design by Zan Fox.

Sunset Books
Editor, David E. Clark
Managing Editor, Elizabeth L. Hogan

Fifth printing June 1986

Contents

Getting Acquainted with Annuals & Perennials

More value for your dollar! Greater performance for its size! Such claims, though typical lures in advertising promotions, can truthfully be made for two general groups of plants: annuals and perennials. These plants, whether measured pound for pound, dollar for dollar, or in terms of value received per square foot of garden occupied, give you the most garden color.

Additionally, annuals can provide your garden with color more quickly than any other plants. By selecting long-blooming annuals and perennials and choosing those that bloom in succession, you can have color for nearly the entire blooming season.

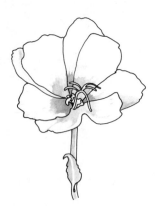

Annuals. A plant that completes its life cycle within a year and then dies is an annual. In nature its life cycle begins at the start of the growing season (usually late winter to early spring) when the seed germinates. The seedling plant rapidly grows large enough to produce flowers. Those flowers, if left on the plant, will set seed. The seed develops and matures on the plants, then falls to the ground. It is then dispersed by wind, birds, or animals, or maybe it is planted. The parent plant dies, but the seed will repeat the cycle in the next growing season.

Most of us are familiar with annuals though we may never have thought to classify them. Marigolds, petunias, and zinnias are annuals; so are the majority of popular vegetables such as beans, corn, and lettuce. Even many weeds are annuals, such as that persistent lawn and garden pest, crabgrass.

Plant breeders are continually working to provide improved annuals for gardeners. Better growth, increased disease resistance, a broader range of colors or patterns, more uniform seedlings, increased weather resistance, and shorter and more compact plants are foremost among their goals. Each year, seed catalogs and nursery seed racks temptingly offer the latest fruits of this labor.

Because the work of plant breeders to produce more uniform plants has given rise to numerous lines of similar-looking plants, we offer some explanation of the terms used to designate similar groups of plants. *Strain* (as in Thumbelina strain zinnias) indicates that the plants have similar growth characteristics, but vary in some particular way, usually color. *Series* has the same implication.

F₁ hybrids result from carefully controlled processes: two inbred strains with particularly desirable characteristics are crossed with one another (usually by hand pollination), and the resulting seeds produce the F₁ hybrid plants. These hybrids will embody desirable characteristics such as vigor and uniform height from each parent strain. But—as opposed to an inbred strain or series—the offspring of F₁ hybrids will not be plants with uniform characteristics.

Tetraploid (usually shortened to Tet or Tetra) plants have twice as many chromosomes as ordinary *diploid* plants. As a result, tetraploid plants have larger flowers with stiffer petals and stems and, frequently, larger leaves.

Perennials. Longevity distinguishes perennials from annuals. Wherever climate and garden conditions are suitable, a perennial will live—growing and blooming each year—for at least three years. What distinguishes perennials from shrubs, on the other hand, is the lack of woody plant parts. You may encounter the term *herbaceous perennial*. Herbaceous means "like an herb" or, simply, "not woody." In the strictest sense these are the perennials that die down to the ground at the end of each growing season, then grow new stems and leaves at the start of the next. Peonies and hostas are typical perennials that disappear completely.

Other perennials, such as Shasta daisies (*Chrysanthemum maximum*) and coral bells (*Heuchera sanguinea*), will go through winter with tufts of foliage, ready to grow and send up flower stalks after cold weather ends. Finally there are truly evergreen perennials—for example, evergreen daylilies (*Hemerocallis*) and lilies-of-the-Nile (*Agapanthus*)—whose plants persist almost unchanged throughout winter.

This brings us to the matter of hardiness. Obviously the plants that disappear above ground, leaving live roots and growth eyes beneath the soil, are in the best position to survive freezing winters. Those that go through their dormancy with tufts of foliage sticking up above the ground may still endure cold winters if they are mulched, particularly if they are covered by snow. But the truly evergreen perennials that remain totally exposed are most susceptible to damage from low temperatures.

This aspect of hardiness prompts us to modify our definition of a perennial to a plant that lives for at least three years *wherever climate and garden conditions are suitable*. A favorite and reliably evergreen perennial in Los Angeles may be able to perform only as an annual in Chicago.

Biennials. Between annuals and perennials lies a small category of plants—biennials—that behave as though they were lazy annuals. Typically, they germinate from seed in spring and devote the first year's growing season to developing the plant. During the second spring or summer, they flower, set seed, and die at the end of that growing season. Foxgloves (*Digitalis*) and Canterbury bells (*Campanula medium*) are two long-time favorites.

Plant breeders have been at work with the most popular of these plants—not only to improve their appearance, as with annuals, but also to develop speeded-up strains that will perform as annuals by completing their growth cycle in one year.

Annuals & perennials then and now

Traditionally, annuals and perennials have been assigned specific—and separate—roles in the garden. This legacy stems from the grand gardens of Victorian and Edwardian times.

In those days, annuals were used strictly for bedding-out: planting in large, uniform masses or in patterns that produced a sort of painting or tapestry of flowers. Thousands of plants of spring-flowering annuals might be set out for an early-season show, then discarded and re-placed by thousands of summer-flowering plants for mid- and late-season color. These displays had such a powerful impact and became so strongly associated with the use of annuals, that today many gardeners still think in terms of planting a bed of annuals—and only annuals.

Turn-of-the-century fashion also determined the role of perennials, so that today we have the legacy of the perennial border. Such a border was usually 6 to 10 feet wide, edged by a lawn or pavement, backed by a tall hedge or wall, and as long as the gardener desired. Perennials that made up the border were planted in complex arrangements of color, leaf texture, height, and season of bloom. The objective was to have a display of bloom from spring through fall, with all plants complementing one another, even when not flowering.

These specific roles—annuals in beds, perennials in borders—are still useful guidelines for planting. You can see large-scale examples of them in some public gardens and on the grounds of some estates that are open to public viewing. Even in today's more compact home gardens, it's possible to plant a dramatic bed of annuals or a pleasing border of perennials. There are other ways to use annuals and perennials, though, and most often they're employed in a variety of situations.

Annuals and perennials together. Even during the time of the grand gardens, annuals and perennials were combined in charming ways in English cottage gardens, as well as in kitchen and cutting gardens of many other nations. There are advantages to this kind of planting. Many annuals have a long flowering period that perennials lack, yet many perennials have interesting leaves or shapes in addition to beautiful blossoms. Combining the two groups can produce a garden that provides color plus interesting detail.

Mixed plantings. In this case, we're talking about a mixture of annuals and perennials with shrubs and trees as well. This practice also goes back to the time of the cottage gardens. Shrubs, such as roses, lavender, sages, rockroses, lilacs, and forsythias, were used for seasonal color. Other combinations included woodland and shade-loving annuals and perennials assorting with flowering cherries, rhododendrons, azaleas, and camellias.

Isolated accents. Perennials are particularly suited for accent-planting, providing spots of interesting color or shape where they can be expected to perform for a number of years without disturbance. The possibilities are nearly endless: a bleeding heart beside a garden pool, a clump of poppies by a garden gate, a mass of daylilies embracing a garden bench, a cluster of forget-me-nots in the dappled shade of a flowering tree, a favorite peony beside a house entry.

In containers. As long as people have grown flowers for pleasure, they've grown flowers in containers as well as in the ground. Modern gardening fashion, however, is making ever greater use of containers of all sorts, including the fixed container known as a raised bed. As yards become smaller and cluster housing becomes more prevalent, container gardening becomes more and more important as a way to increase garden space. And for the apartment dweller, containers may offer the only opportunity to have any garden at all. As bountiful providers of color, annuals and perennials stand out as first choice for container planting.

Steps to Success: Planting & Care

Success in the garden can be defined as results that meet or exceed your expectations. It's easier to achieve such success if you begin your efforts with some basic knowledge. So in this chapter you'll find the fundamentals, starting with the preparatory steps on pages 6–9 and continuing through points of routine care on pages 9–15.

Annuals and perennials encompass so large and diverse a group of plants that it's impossible to generalize completely. As much as possible, though, we've emphasized the similarities in basic culture for these two plant groups and pointed out differences or exceptions where they occur.

Where to Plant

Success begins with a decision. Some gardeners first choose the plants they want to grow, then select suitable places to grow them. But most gardeners think of location first, specific plants second. The main point is that any site must provide the proper conditions for the plants you select for it. Nothing will thwart success in your garden as much as mismatching plants and growing conditions.

Most of the popular annuals and perennials need sunshine and good soil. For shaded locations or for soils that are dry, extra moist, or nutrient-poor, the range of plant choices is somewhat limited. And it's probably safe to say that none of the annuals and perennials described in this book will thrive in dense shade or in soils heavily infiltrated by roots of trees and shrubs. Where soil is poor or full of roots but other conditions are favorable, consider growing plants in containers, planters, or raised beds (see page 13). Remember, too, that the more you can enjoy the success of your garden, the sweeter it will be; so plant your annuals and perennials where you can see them most often.

When to Plant

To prepare soil in advance of planting, you need to know the best times for setting out annuals and perennials.

Annuals

When to set out annuals or sow seeds depends on your climate and growing season.

Cold-winter climates. In much of the country where winters are snowy or at least freezing, annuals bloom from late spring through early autumn. If you're going to start plants from seeds,start them indoors so the seedlings will be ready to go outdoors as soon as frost danger is past. If you plan to sow seeds in the open ground, it's important to do it right after danger of hard frost is over (see chart on Average Hard-frost Dates, page 7).

Seedlings of hardy and early-blooming annuals, especially, should be set out as soon as danger of severe frost is over to give them the longest possible growing season. This means you should prepare the soil as soon as it becomes workable in late winter or early spring.

If you delay planting until weather has settled into mid-spring warmth, you risk disappointment. Annuals that are set out too late struggle to establish roots and grow at the same time, giving a second-rate show because they never achieve full growth.

Mild-winter climates. Where winters are mild—either frost-free or lightly frosty—early spring is the time for setting out the late spring and summer-flowering annuals.

But there is another annual season in these mild climate areas: winter. For flowering winter treats such as cinerarias, Iceland poppies, and calendulas, to name a few, set out plants in early autumn while the days are still warm enough to encourage growth, but daylight time is decreasing. Aim to get the plants off to a good start during the waning warmth of autumn so they will be husky enough to give good bloom during the short days of winter. Caution—if winter annuals are set out too soon, while days are warm or hot and longer than nights, these plants may rush to bloom far too soon on poorly established plants.

Perennials

Wherever you live, you can follow a convenient rule-of-thumb for planting perennials. In spring, plant perennials that bloom in summer or autumn. In early autumn, plant perennials that bloom in spring. This is the rule if you are planting perennials that have been dug from established clumps and sold bare root. (If you have ordered perennials from reputable mail-order nurseries, they will send the plants at the proper planting times.)

If you set out perennials that have been grown in containers, you can do it at any time of year. However, common sense suggests that you should not plant perennials during the most intense heat of summer or, in the cold-winter areas of the country, in late autumn just before the onset of severe winter weather.

Soil Sense

Annuals have only a short lifetime in which to become established and to grow and bloom. A well-prepared soil will enhance the productiveness of that lifetime. And perennials, because they remain in the same soil for a period of years, benefit from thorough preparation of the soil that must sustain them.

A good garden soil is porous and drains well, yet retains sufficient moisture for roots. Also, it provides ample nutrients to meet the needs of plants. Preparing such a soil is one of the main tasks of a gardener.

Acid or alkaline: testing your soil

A soil test is not always a necessary procedure, but one that may materially aid your success in the garden. Typically, such a test will reveal the acidity or alkalinity of your soils (expressed in pH numbers: pH 7 is neutral, pH greater than 7 is alkaline, pH less than 7 is acid). The test can also point out any deficiencies of major nutrients. (As a rule of thumb, high-rainfall areas tend to have acid soils, low-rainfall areas have alkaline soils).

Professional soil laboratories will test your soil for a fee (see the Yellow Pages of your telephone directory for listings). Also, kits that let you do your own testing are sold through mail-order garden supply companies and in some nurseries.

If the soil test indicates that your soil is too acidic, add lime when you prepare the soil (see below). If the test shows that your soil is too alkaline, you can add sulfur, iron sulfate, or a similar substance. A local nurseryman, a soil-testing laboratory, or your County Cooperative Extension Advisor (agricultural advisor) can tell you how much to add. If the test shows that your soil is deficient in one or more nutrients, add the appropriate fertilizer (see page 10) when you prepare the soil.

Improving your soil structure

Thorough preparation means digging and turning the soil to a

Average Hard-Frost Dates*

Based on U.S.D.A. weather records

State	Last in Spring	First in Fall	State	Last in Spring	First in Fall	State	Last in Spring	First in Fall
Alabama, N.W.	Mar. 25	Oct. 30	Kansas	Apr. 20	Oct. 15	Ohio, No.	May 6	Oct. 15
Alabama, S.E.	Mar. 8	Nov. 15	Kentucky	Apr. 15	Oct. 20	Ohio, So.	Apr. 20	Oct. 20
Arizona, No.	Apr. 23	Oct. 19				Oklahoma	Apr. 2	Nov. 2
Arizona, So.	Mar. 1	Dec. 1	Louisiana, No.	Mar. 13	Nov. 10	Oregon, W.	Apr. 17	Oct. 25
Arkansas, No.	Apr. 7	Oct. 23	Louisiana, So.	Feb. 20	Nov. 20	Oregon, E.	June 4	Sept. 22
Arkansas, So.	Mar. 25	Nov. 3						
			Maine	May 25	Sept. 25	Pennsylvania, W.	Apr. 20	Oct. 10
California			Maryland	Apr. 19	Oct. 20	Pennsylvania, Cen.	May 1	Oct. 15
Imperial Valley	Jan. 25	Dec. 15	Massachusetts	Apr. 25	Oct. 25	Pennsylvania, E.	Apr. 17	Oct. 15
Interior Valley	Mar. 1	Nov. 15	Michigan, Upper Pen.	May 25	Sept. 15			
Southern Coast	Jan. 15	Dec. 15	Michigan, No.	May 17	Sept. 25	Rhode Island	Apr. 25	Oct. 25
Central Coast	Feb. 25	Dec. 1	Michigan, So.	May 10	Oct. 8			
Mountain Sections	Apr. 25	Sept. 1	Minnesota, No.	May 25	Sept. 15	S. Carolina, N.W.	Apr. 1	Nov. 8
Colorado, West	May 25	Sept. 18	Minnesota, So.	May 11	Oct. 1	S. Carolina, S.E.	Mar. 15	Nov. 15
Colorado, N.E.	May 11	Sept. 27	Mississippi, No.	Mar. 25	Oct. 30	S. Dakota	May 15	Sept. 25
Colorado, S.E.	May 1	Oct. 15	Mississippi, So.	Mar. 15	Nov. 15			
Connecticut	Apr. 25	Oct. 20	Missouri	Apr. 20	Oct. 20	Tennessee	Apr. 10	Oct. 25
			Montana	May 21	Sept. 22	Texas, N.W.	Mar. 21	Nov. 10
Delaware	Apr. 15	Oct. 25				Texas, N.E.	Apr. 15	Nov. 1
District of Columbia	Apr. 11	Oct. 23	Nebraska, W.	May 11	Oct. 4	Texas, So.	Feb. 10	Dec. 15
			Nebraska, E.	Apr. 15	Oct. 15			
Florida, No.	Feb. 25	Dec. 5	Nevada, W.	May 19	Sept. 22	Utah	Apr. 26	Oct. 19
Florida, Cen.	Feb. 11	Dec. 28	Nevada, E.	June 1	Sept. 14			
Florida, South of Lake Okeechobee, almost frost-free			New Hampshire	May 23	Sept. 25	Vermont	May 23	Sept. 25
			New Jersey	Apr. 20	Oct. 25	Virginia, No.	Apr. 15	Oct. 25
Georgia, No.	Apr. 1	Nov. 1	New Mexico, No.	Apr. 23	Oct. 17	Virginia, So.	Apr. 10	Oct. 30
Georgia, So.	Mar. 15	Nov. 15	New Mexico, So.	Apr. 1	Nov. 1			
			New York, W.	May 10	Oct. 8	Washington, W.	Apr. 10	Nov. 15
Idaho	May 21	Sept. 22	New York, E.	May 1	Oct. 15	Washington, E.	May 15	Oct. 1
Illinois, No.	May 1	Oct. 8	New York, No.	May 15	Oct. 1	West Virginia, W.	May 1	Oct. 15
Illinois, So.	Apr. 15	Oct. 20	N. Carolina, W.	Apr. 15	Oct. 25	West Virginia, E.	May 15	Oct. 1
Indiana, No.	May 1	Oct. 8	N. Carolina, E.	Apr. 8	Nov. 1	Wisconsin, No.	May 17	Sept. 25
Indiana, So.	Apr. 15	Oct. 20	N. Dakota, W.	May 21	Sept. 13	Wisconsin, So.	May 1	Oct. 10
Iowa, No.	May 1	Oct. 2	N. Dakota, E.	May 16	Sept. 20	Wyoming, W.	June 20	Aug. 20
Iowa, So.	Apr. 15	Oct. 9				Wyoming, E.	May 21	Sept. 20

*Allow 10 days either side of above dates to meet local conditions and seasonal differences.

depth of about 12 inches. For a small area, hand digging with a spade or spading fork is best. Large open areas can be prepared with a rotary tiller.

Soil is in good condition for digging when it is moist, yet lumps of it crumble easily. Never work a soil that is saturated with water and sticky; this only compacts the soil—just the opposite of what you're trying to achieve.

After you have dug the ground, broken up clods, and generally loosened and aerated the soil, add the organic amendments (see below) and thoroughly dig or till them in. Be generous—spread about a 3-inch layer over the soil and work it in thoroughly. At the same time add a fertilizer and any materials needed to adjust the pH of the soil.

Soil amendments. Many sorts of organic soil amendments are available at nurseries and garden centers: steer manure, peat moss, and various wood by-products (some simply labeled

"garden compost"), just to name a few. Regional agriculture may produce by-products that could be used—ground corncobs, grape or apple pomace, rice hulls, or mushroom compost.

If you use a wood by-product, be sure that it's labeled "nitrogen fortified" or "nitrogen stabilized," or is well decomposed. The organisms that break down organic materials require nitrogen to do their work. Most organic soil amendments contain enough nitrogen to supply those organisms, but raw wood by-products—and any high cellulose material—are deficient in nitrogen unless it had been added. Whenever the organic material doesn't contain enough nitrogen to satisfy the decay organisms, they will draw out available nitrogen from the soil, possibly at the expense of your plants' growth.

Fertilizer. Also, when you dig in the organic amendments, incorporate a complete fertilizer

(see "Nutrients & Fertilizers," page 10) that has a lot of phosphorous and potassium—a 5-10-10 formula, for example.

If possible, prepare your soil several weeks before you intend to plant. This will give soil and amendments some time to mellow and settle slightly. During this period various weeds may appear and you can pull or hoe them out without having to work around newly set plants. Then, just before planting, you can do a final raking to smooth out the humps and hollows.

Planting

You can start most annuals and perennials from either seeds or plants. It's mostly a matter of preference, but cost is a factor.

Adventurous, curious, or ardent gardeners may prefer to raise annuals and some perennials from seed. There is enormous satisfaction in being able

Starting with Seeds

Many annuals and perennials are easy to grow from seed if you pay attention to several factors.

Timing: Most seed packages specify when to sow seeds outdoors. But if you like, you can sow seeds indoors in flats or small containers a few weeks before you plan to transplant seedlings into the garden.

Use a seed-starting soil mixture that is sterile, such as a packaged kind. Also use clean pots, flats, starting pots, or other containers. (Wash old containers with a dilute solution of bleach and rinse well.)

Proper planting depth is important, too. Carefully follow directions on the seed package and cover seeds with soil.

Water consistently and gently. Seedlings will perish quickly from too much or too little water, so check soil moisture twice a day.

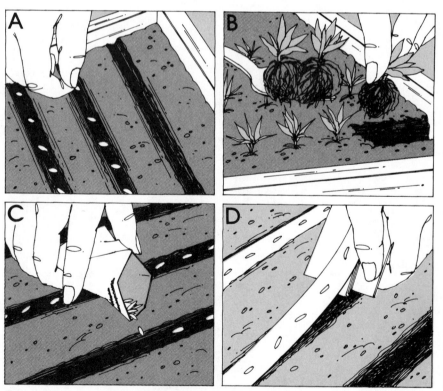

Sow seeds in flat (A) to transplant (B) to garden or pots; or sow seeds in garden from packet (C) or tape (D).

to look at a plant and say, "I grew it myself." Unquestionably, too, a greater variety of annuals and perennials is available in seed packets offered by commercial companies than in the form of started plants at the local nursery or garden center. For directions on how to raise plants from seed, see page 8.

Nowadays, though, probably more gardeners and would-be gardeners choose to set out young nursery plants—predominantly annuals—rather than sow packets of seeds. Usually these young plants are available at the earliest planting time.

A limited variety of perennials growing in 1 or 2-gallon containers may be found at nurseries and garden centers, but a far greater selection is available by mail order from specialty growers. These plants are shipped totally bare-root or with roots packed in a moist material to prevent their drying out.

Simple planting procedures

It's important to set a plant at its proper depth to ensure that its roots can spread into the soil. You also want to be sure the soil is settled and firm around the roots, leaving no air pockets. Dig the planting hole larger than the plant's root-ball. If you're setting out plants from flats and containers, be sure the tops of the root-balls are even with the surface of the soil. If you are setting out a bare-root plant, form a mound of soil in the planting hole and spread roots over the mound; make sure that the plant's crown (where roots join leaves or growing point) will be just at soil surface. In all cases, firm the soil around the roots and water well.

Watering

"How much.... How often....?" The answers to these questions about watering depend on the needs of your plants and the environmental factors that influence water use. The following guidelines should help you.

Guidelines for watering

The oft-repeated advice is this: water thoroughly—and infrequently. "Thoroughly" means watering deeply enough to moisten all of the roots. Deep watering promotes deep-growing roots because roots seek moisture. If the water goes deep, so will the roots. And the deeper the roots go, the less vulnerable they are to moisture fluctuations at the soil surface. If you water plants lightly, and daily, they'll establish shallow root systems and be vulnerable to sudden drying out, which can happen even in the most carefully tended gardens.

How often you may need to water depends on two factors: the sort of soil you have and the weather. The illustrations below show clay (small particles close together), sand (large particles with big pore spaces), and loam (a mixture of particle sizes) soils.

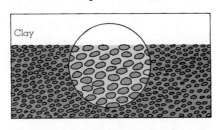

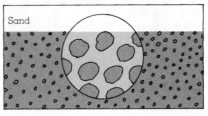

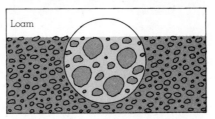

Clay soil drains slowly, holds much water; sandy soil drains fast, holds little water; loam is in between

A plant takes in moisture through its roots and gives off moisture through its leaves—a process called transpiration. Weather influences watering frequency because it affects a plant's transpiration rate. On windy or hot dry days, a plant's transpiration rate increases; leaves lose moisture faster. A point may even come when the plant's roots can't get water from the soil as fast as the plant needs it. Then the plant wilts. Conversely, on overcast or windless days, a plant's transpiration rate is slower.

Day length also affects transpiration simply because there are more or fewer hours of sunlight, and perhaps wind, to act upon the plants. The size of a plant influences its rate of water consumption, too. Newly set out annuals, for example, won't draw nearly as much water from the soil as they will when they're full size. In fact, newly planted plants need a close water watch because their small root systems are in the top few inches of soil which can dry out quickly. Later, when plants are larger and better established (have deeper roots), you may not need to water them until the top inch or two of soil is dry.

In general, annuals and perennials have slightly different watering requirements.

Annuals. To produce first-class results, these short-lived plants must grow continuously and without stopping. This means they need adequate moisture throughout their growing and blooming periods: enough water so the plants never wilt, but not so much that the soil remains saturated and the roots drown.

Perennials. Like annuals, these long-lived plants need regular moisture from the moment they begin growing until they are through flowering in order to develop.

Unlike annuals, which die after they have finished blooming and have produced their seeds, perennials build up reserves of nutrients for the next year's performance before they go into a period of dormancy. (Dormancy for perennials can involve anything from the loss of leaves to cessation of growth). Perennials, then, need regular watering for a period following bloom until they enter their dormant or resting state.

Once perennials become dormant, some will tolerate routine watering, others prefer or actually require much less. The water requirements for annuals and perennials are given in the individual plant descriptions in the A–Z listings on pages 64–94.

Mulches

A mulch is usually a layer of an organic substance on the soil surface. It acts as an insulating blanket to shield the soil from the drying action of sun and wind. It saves you from having to water as often. It also keeps the soil surface from being compacted by watering, and keeps the soil underneath more permeable to water. A final benefit is the gradual but continuous breakdown of the mulch material in contact with the soil. This means the mulch is constantly contributing the benefits of decaying organic matter to the soil.

A good mulch should not pack down so tightly that it prevents water from penetrating it; and it should not be so light or loose that the wind will blow it away. A mulch should also look reasonably attractive and not cost too much.

Animal manures (well rotted, not fresh) and compost make very good mulches. You can also use various residues of agricultural processing, such as ground corncobs, cotton gin trash, and apple and grape pomace. Wood by-products like chips and bark are attractive and fairly long lasting; but sawdust is too fine to be satisfactory. Peat moss may

be suitable while it's moist, but when it's dry it repels water and is easily blown about. Grass clippings will work if you apply them in a thin layer and allow them to dry before applying another thin layer. Piled on thickly, though, they will become compacted. If you don't mind the appearance, pulled weeds, especially grassy ones, also make a fine mulch.

To be sure your mulch is effective, you should apply it in a layer 1 to 2 inches deep. For annuals, spread mulch between plants, bringing it near to their bases but not covering them. It's best to mulch perennials between clumps, leaving their centers open to air.

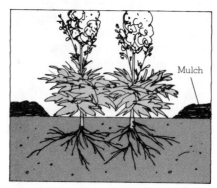

Layer of mulch 1–2 inches thick reduces moisture loss from soil. Keep mulch from bases of plants.

In hot weather, a mulch keeps the soil temperature desirably cool. But applied too early in the season, when soil is cold, a mulch will delay warming of the soil and slow down development of plants. Particularly in cold-winter climates where you need to make the most of the growing season, don't apply a mulch until spring weather has taken winter's chill from the ground.

Nutrients & Fertilizers

For their best development and continuing health, plants need adequate nutrients, most of which they extract from the soil. But if the soil doesn't provide enough nutrients, you, the gardener, must step in and apply

fertilizers (popularly termed "plant food") to supplement the nutrient supply.

Newly planted annuals and perennials especially need a steady and balanced diet to reach a healthy, robust maturity. Three nutrients—nitrogen, phosphorus, and potassium— are needed in the largest quantities. Then there are about six minor nutrients that are vital, but needed in far smaller amounts. Various trace elements are also required, but in minute quantities. Here are the three major nutrients that plants get from the soil.

Nitrogen promotes rapid growth, particularly of leaves and stems. In nature, nitrogen comes primarily from decaying organic matter. It's almost always in short supply, though.

Nitrogen is also available to plant roots through soluble chemical compounds in the soil solution. This form of nitrogen, though, is easily leached from the soil. It's easy to understand, then, why nitrogen is the nutrient that gardeners most often need to supply to plants.

Phosphorus regulates growth, encourages early root development and, hence, nutrient uptake. It also promotes flower and seed production. Phosphorus is often present in soil in adequate supply. In distinctly acid soils, though, it may be unavailable to plant roots because of a chemical reaction caused by the acidity. Raising the soil's pH (see "Testing Your Soil," page 7) may make enough phosphorus available to your plants, though.

Phosphorus is not subject to leaching. Instead, it is slowly but steadily released in compounds into the soil solution where roots can assimilate it. Because of its low solubility and the fact that it must form soluble compounds in order to be available to roots, phosphorus fertilizers are most effective when incorporated into the soil before planting. For established perennials, however, you have no choice but to give supplemental phosphorus by surface applications scratched into the soil.

Potassium plays a part in the production of a plant's sugars and starches, and in the production of cellulose which contributes to the strength of plant tissues. Potash is the compound through which potassium usually becomes available to plants. Even though it's very soluble, the potassium from this compound is not usually taken up by the roots via the soil solution. Instead, some of the soluble potash that is applied to the soil in fertilizer joins a small portion of the soil's usually great store of potassium in a form called exchangeable potassium. The roots pick up this exchangeable potassium from direct contact with particles of clay and organic matter rather than by assimilation of the soil solution. Before planting you can apply dry fertilizer with potassium to the soil. After planting you can water-in fertilizer with potassium in solution.

These three major nutrients, when combined into one commercial fertilizer, constitute what is called a complete fertilizer. You will usually find the percentages of these nutrients listed on the fertilizer package, and expressed in numbers such as 5–10–5. Translated, this means the fertilizer contains 5% nitrogen; 10% phosphorus, and 5% potassium; and the numbers

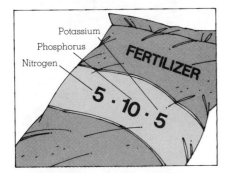

Fertilizer label specifies percentages of nitrogen, phosphorus, and potassium –in that order –contained in package.

always refer to the nutrients in that order.

Fertilizer choices

Most gardeners prefer the convenience of complete fertilizers. But you can also buy each of the major nutrients separately, such as blood meal for nitrogen, bone meal for phosphorus, and ground rock potash for potassium. Before you proceed to the fertilizer section of the local nursery, though, there's more to know about available types.

Dry and liquid. The boxes and bags of fertilizers on the nursery shelf contain dry fertilizers. Many are complete fertilizers, in granular or pellet form, that dissolve over a period of time when mixed into the soil or applied to the surface. Some dry fertilizers are single-nutrient types that are also to be mixed into the soil or applied to its surface.

Bottles of liquid fertilizers and containers of soluble granules are meant to be dissolved in water (according to label directions) and added to the soil. Liquids may also be complete-fertilizer or single-nutrient types (usually nitrogen sources, such as fish emulsion).

When preparing the soil for annuals or perennials, dry fertilizers are an obvious choice. Most gardeners prefer to continue with dry fertilizers as they are needed during the growing season (see "Timing and Applications," below) because they are relatively quick and simple to use.

Liquid fertilizers, however, are deservedly popular for container-grown annuals and perennials. Where roots are confined in containers and water can reach all the roots in a matter of minutes, liquid fertilizers can act as quick tonics. Even though nutrients not taken up immediately by the roots will be quickly leached out by subsequent waterings, it is little extra trouble to mix and use liquid fertilizers repeatedly during a growing season as you

water the containers. Liquid fertilizers can be just as effective for plants in the ground, but unless you have just a small planting, you'll probably find them less convenient to use than dry kinds.

Slow-release. Gaining in popularity and availability are various dry fertilizers that categorically are termed slow, controlled, or timed-release. In one way or another, these fertilizers resist or control the leaching of nutrients by water. One application will slowly but steadily release nutrients with each watering over a matter of months. The chief benefit of these fertilizers, though, is sustained release of nitrogen—the most-needed major nutrient and the one that is the most easily leached from the soil. And while they cost more than other kinds of fertilizers, this is balanced out by the reduced amount you use in a given season as well as by the time you save.

The forerunner of these fertilizers was the urea-formaldehyde type (called urea or urea-form) which gave a sustained nitrogen release because it broke down slowly in the soil. Any fertilizer that contains nitrogen in the form of urea (this will be stated on the back of the package) will give a more sustained nitrogen release than fertilizers that contain nitrogen in the nitrate or ammoniac form.

A more recent development in slow-release fertilizers is the type in which nutrient granules are encased in plastic coating. This permits the nutrients to diffuse over a long period of time.

Directions on the packages of slow-release fertilizers clearly state the amounts to use and length of effectiveness. These fertilizers are equally popular for plants growing in the ground and in containers.

Timing the applications

When do you apply fertilizer? The answer depends upon the

general kind of plant as well as the time in the growing season.

Annuals come into your garden as small plants with small root systems. Both roots and tops have to grow rapidly in order to produce the results you expect. Therefore, you need to ensure a steady supply of nutrients from planting time through blooming time. If you added a complete fertilizer when you prepared the soil, there should be enough nutrients to keep plants growing vigorously for about the first 6 weeks. At that point, you should apply a further nutrient boost—dry, liquid, or slow-release. Thereafter, how often you continue to fertilize depends on the kind of fertilizer you plan to use.

Liquids should be repeated about every two weeks (or every 7 to 10 days at half-strength). How often you should apply a dry fertilizer depends on its strength; the package directions will suggest timing and quantity. As for slow-release fertilizers, one application may be enough where growing seasons are fairly short; use no more than two applications where growing seasons are long.

Perennials live over from one year to the next, so they have established roots. They also have the ability to store nutrients in their stems and roots. As a result, they have a head start over annuals at the beginning of a growing season and are ready to respond with vigor to the stimulus of growing-season weather. Perennials benefit most from two fertilizer applications each year. Give the first application as they begin their year's growth. At this time they need nitrogen in particular, so choose a fertilizer with a fair amount of nitrogen—5 to 10 percent—such as 5–10–5 or 10–10–10.

After blooming—and even perennials grown primarily for foliage have a bloom season— your perennials will need nutrients again so that they can make offsets, put on additional growth,

and store nutrients to prepare for the next year's performance. Repeat the application of the fertilizer that was used earlier in the year, in amounts suggested in the directions on the label.

Maintaining Appearances

If good care accounts for 80 percent of a successful garden, the other 20 percent can be attributed to good garden grooming. Here are four tips on how to "keep up appearances" in your garden.

Weeding. A hard fact of life is that where there are gardens there will be weeds. (A weed in a garden is any plant that is both unintended and unwanted.) Preparing the soil well in advance of planting time (see page 7). gives you the chance to grub out the first weeds to sprout. Also a mulch (see page 10) will suppress the germination of weed seeds in the soil and make it easier to pull weeds that sprout.

Pull weeds when the soil is moist but not sloppy wet. Soil that is in good condition for digging (see page 7) is right for weeding. Be sure to pull out the roots of the weeds and not just pull off the leafy tops; many weeds resprout from their roots unless you pull them up.

Pinching. Left to their own devices, some annuals and perennials tend to become sprawly, floppy, top-heavy, or leggy. In many instances you can counteract these tendencies by pinching (see illustration above). In plants that tend to grow long stems instead of branching ones, pinching will force branching from growth buds along the stems. The result will be a denser, more compact plant. Chrysanthemums, marguerites, pelargoniums, and petunias are among the familiar plants that can be beneficially fattened up in this manner.

Promote bushiness of plants and increase their flowers by pinching off growing tips early in season.

Staking. The purpose of staking is obvious: to keep plants, especially tall, blooming plants, from falling over. Some flowers, such as delphiniums, almost always need staking because their blossoming stems are too top-heavy to stand erect. Other plants may require assistance occasionally if, for example, too much nitrogen and/or too much water causes them to grow long but weak stems. There are still other plants that are by nature somewhat sprawly or inclined to fall away from the center when they're blooming. They can be kept fairly compact by using stakes or wire to encircle them. The illustrations below show various staking methods.

Help flowers with spindly stems stay upright by using stakes and twine, wire rings, or soft plant ties.

Remember that the most effective staking not only keeps plants upright, but also is unobtrusive. Your eye can be distracted from a gorgeous blossom if an unattractive pole is holding it up.

Deadheading. Nature's purpose for flowers is the production of seeds to ensure perpetuation of the plant. In many plants, once the first blooms begin to form seeds, the plants' energies are put into developing seeds rather than producing more flowers. Removing spent flowers, called deadheading, can do more than keep a garden neat; it can keep it blooming.

Not all annuals and perennials respond to deadheading with prolonged bloom, though. Bearded irises and peonies, for example, will not produce additional flowering stems just because you remove old blossoms. But marigolds and poppies, to cite two, will give you a longer flowering period if you remove spent blooms. In fact it is wise to remove the spent flower or entire flower spikes of any perennial that typically sets a crop of seeds following bloom. This way the plant's energies will be used for growth instead of seed production.

Special Care for Perennials

Up to this point we have discussed the similarities in caring for annuals and perennials. But there are some additional steps that must be taken with perennials because they go on living year after year.

Yearly cleanup

Some time after blooming season, perennials need to be cleaned up. Some remain green and attractive throughout the growing season, so you just need to remove their old flowering stems when they finish blooming. Many perennials, though, go partially or completely dormant and lose part or all of their leaves and stems. Both for appearance and plant health, you should remove the old stems and dead plant growth. Dead leaves that collect at the base of a plant or clump can harbor pests (especially slugs and snails) and may provide a source of fungus-disease reinfection the next year. If left in place through winter rain or snow, dead leaves may pack down into a decaying mat that could rot the plant.

Winter protection

Gardeners in the coldest parts of the country often count on a thick blanket of snow to keep their perennials snugly protected for winter. But sometimes

Annuals & Perennials in Containers

Many annuals and some perennials grow happily in pots, tubs, and planter boxes. These containers can bring beautiful flowers to places where you couldn't grow them ordinarily: patios, decks, porches, window boxes, even the space above ground that's filled with competing tree and shrub roots.

For real success with plants in containers, you must prepare the soil with extra care. For example, ordinary soil in a container can become a sodden lump when wet, and a bricklike one when dry. You need a permeable soil for roots to grow well.

If you're planting just a few small containers, you may want to purchase packaged planting (or potting) mix and use it directly from the bag. But if you're planting many or large containers, or if you just prefer to do it yourself, you may concoct your own potting mixture. For home use, a time-tested basic mix combines 2 parts good garden soil (*not* heavy clay), 1 part perlite or sand (river or builder's sand), and 1 part peat moss or some other organic material (but not manure).

Because a container is exposed to the drying action of sun and wind, you'll have to water container plants more often than you water the same plants in the ground. With your fingers, check container-soil moisture; water thoroughly when soil feels dry beneath the soil's surface. Thorough watering means applying water to *all* the container's soil: completely wet the surface and let the water flow through the soil and out the drainage holes.

Unfortunately, thorough watering flushes nutrients out of the container soil, so to get exurberant growth you must supplement your plants' nutrient supply. Dry granular fertilizers, slow-release fertilizers, and liquid formulations are your choices. See pages 10–12 for a discussion of fertilizers.

Good size drain hole in container is crucial to success of most container-grown plants.

they cover the plants with a light layer of straw or hay before the snows arrive. The danger zones for many basically hardy perennials, though, are the parts of the country where snow cover is not reliable, where several cycles of freezing and thawing may occur during winter.

In these regions, gardeners routinely protect many of their perennials with an insulating blanket of some organic material that won't compact. Rather than keeping the plants warm, the idea is to keep them frozen, but not so cold that they're killed. Straw, evergreen boughs, salt hay, or marsh hay are the materials traditionally favored for such winter protection. Wait until a hard frost has frozen the soil, then apply a covering of salt hay or straw about 6 inches deep, or of evergreen boughs in two layers with the top layer at right angles to the bottom.

Timing the removal of protection depends entirely on the particular year's weather. You want to remove the protective covering before perennials start to put on much growth, but not so soon that any emerging growth would be killed by late freezes. To some extent you can be guided by the chart on page 7 that lists average dates for the last hard frost in various parts of the country. Remove the covering in two

After ground has frozen, cover perennials with pine branches to protect them from winter damage.

Make cuttings from tips of stems—3 to 4 inches. Dip stem in rooting hormone, then put in pot of rooting soil.

stages, half at a time, to safeguard against surprise late freezes. Established local nursery people—and experience —can give you guidance as to when to remove the covering.

Rejuvenation & propagation

Perennials vary greatly in the length of time they can grow vigorously in one spot without revitalization. Individual plant descriptions in the A–Z listing, pages 64–94, tells you approximately how long you can expect various perennials to grow without revitalizing. But you can be on the lookout for typical signs of decline: smaller flowers and shorter stalks, reduced vigor, overcrowded clumps, centers of clumps bare with live plants around the edges, and, finally, fewer flowers or no flowers.

Although there are perennials (peonies, for example) that grow well in one location for longer than your lifetime, most perennials need periodic rejuvenation in order to continue producing top-quality flowers. You can rejuvenate most perennials by digging up the clump and separating it into single plants or smaller groups of plants. For some short-lived perennials, though, you can only start new plants by taking stem or root cuttings, or beginning with seeds.

The best time to dig and divide perennials is during their dormant season when disturbing

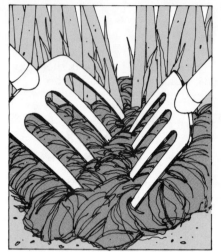

Divide large, clumping perennials such as daylilies by splitting them apart with spading forks.

the roots is least harmful. In general, it's best to divide spring-flowering perennials in summer or autumn, summer and autumn-blooming perennials in early spring just before, or as soon as, growth begins for the year. Specific information is given in the individual plant descriptions on pages 64–94. The above illustrations show how to divide big clumps of perennials, and how to make rooted stem cuttings.

Your efforts will produce not only rejuvenated plants but increased numbers of plants that you can use in your garden or share with friends. If you can't immediately plant these divisions, pot them in individual containers or heel them into the ground. For heeling in, choose a shaded location and cover the plants' roots with soil, sawdust, ground bark, or any material that you can keep moistened (but not saturated). This will keep roots plump and healthy until you can set out the divisions in the garden.

We should point out here that overcrowding is not the only cause of a perennial's decline in vigor. In time the soil itself needs rejuvenation, too. If you plan to replant a perennial in the spot where it has been growing, replenish the soil by digging in organic matter and fertilizer (see page 8).

Common Pests & Plant Diseases

The best way to deal with plant pests and diseases is preventive: keep your garden clean, maintain good soil, give plants their preferred growing conditions, and water and fertilize them as needed. If pests do strike, take prompt measures to thwart their buildup. If diseases appear, treat promptly or remove and destroy affected plants or plant parts. Below we list the most common pests and diseases that may affect some annuals and perennials, plus some controls and preventive measures. Try physical and live controls first; if those fail, use packaged controls.

Pests

Aphids. Soft, round, pinhead to matchhead-size insects live and feed in colonies and stunt plant growth. Usually green or reddish black, sometimes winged.
Physical controls: Use water jet, or wash off with soapy solution.
Live controls: Lacewing larvae.
Packaged controls: Diazinon, malathion, pyrethrins.

Geranium budworms. Larvae of night-flying moths threaten geraniums, ageratums, and petunias. The small, rust-colored or green-striped caterpillars eat holes in buds or unfolded leaves.
Physical controls: Hand pick or destroy hole-ridden flowers.
Live controls: Trichogramma wasps (release right after full moon—when moths mate and lay eggs—to destroy eggs), lacewing larvae (release a week after full moon to ear young larvae).
Packaged controls: Bacillus thuringiensis, diazinon.

Mites. Tiny spiders appear as specks of red, yellow, or green dust, and form silvery webs on undersides of leaves.
Physical controls: Water jet, or wash undersides of leaves with soapy solution 3 days in a row or every other day for a week.
Live controls: Lacewing larvae, mite-eating mites (*Phytoseiulus persimilis*).
Packaged controls: Kelthane, systemic insecticides.

Slugs, snails. Very common, destructive garden pests. They feed at night and on cool, overcast days; on warm sunny days, they hide. Both eat leaves.
Physical controls: Hand pick; or place boards out at night, turn each morning, and squash snails.
Packaged controls: Metaldehyde bait.

White flies. Tiny white, flying pests that attach and feed on undersides of leaves. Nymphs suck plant juices.
Physical controls: Colored cards (greenish yellow cards work best) smeared with a sticky insect-catching material; or wash plants with soapy water.
Live controls: Eggs of *Encarsia formosa* (a whitefly-killing wasp), shoofly plant (*Nicandra*).
Packaged controls: Diazinon, malathion, methoxychlor, nicotine sulfate, systemics.

Beetles. Various hard-shell insects (shell is hard outer wings over soft inner ones) that chew holes in foliage, flowers. Larval phase is grubs (worms) that live in soil. Japanese beetles (½-inch, shiny copper body) and cucumber or diabrotica beetles (¼-inch, yellow with black spots) are very destructive.
Physical controls: Hand pick and destroy beetles.
Packaged controls: Sevin, methoxychlor, malathion; milky spore disease for Japanese beetle grubs.

Diseases

Anthracnose. Fungi infecting leaves and tender shoots as they emerge; most severe in wet spring. Large reddish-brown blotches appear on older leaves.
Physical controls: Collect and burn infected parts.
Packaged controls: Benomyl, Bordeaux, ferbam, fixed copper, folpet, lime sulfur, thiram, zineb.
Preventive measures: Thorough winter cleanup of dead leaves and stems from year's growth.

Botrytis. Gray mold widespread in cool, humid areas. Symptoms are soft, tan to brown spots or blotches on flowers and leaves, followed by covering of coarse gray mold.
Physical contols: Remove and burn infected parts or plants.
Packaged controls: Benomyl, folpet, zineb.
Preventive measures: Avoid overcrowding and damp, shady locations. Give winter cleanup.

Powdery mildew. White or gray, powdery or mealy coating on leaves and flower buds.
Physical controls: Discard badly affected annuals; trim diseased parts of perennials.
Packaged controls: Acti-dione, benomyl, folpet, karathane, sulfur.
Preventive measures: Avoid overcrowding and damp, shady locations. Avoid watering in late afternoon and evening.

Rust. Usually appears first on underside of leaves. Yellow-orange colored pustules mature and burst; wind and splashing water scatter spores.
Physical controls: Discard infected leaves.
Packaged controls: Folpet, zineb, ferbam, sulfur.
Preventive measures: Thorough winter cleanup.

A Colorful Bouquet of Flower Garden Ideas

At your disposal is a diverse assortment of annuals and perennials that can electrify your garden, whatever its size, with color. For truly satisfying results, though, it is important to understand how these plants and their colors can work best for you. In this chapter we describe the ways colors can be combined to maximize your satisfaction. Then we show these plants at work. Also, we show how plants perform in mixed bouquets and wildflower plantings, and we provide charts to tell you what plants to use at different seasons and in various locations.

Using Color Effectively

Well-grown annuals and perennials can furnish plenty of color for your garden, but for greatest impact, you, the gardener, must skillfully combine the colors available. The safest scheme, of course, is monochrome: an all-white garden, a solid bed of yellow marigolds, a planting of only blue irises. But the danger of *monochrome plantings* is monotony. Plants offer vivid opportunities that deserve to be exploited fearlessly—and the best antidote to timidity in combining color is a basic knowledge of color principles.

Understanding the color wheel

The color wheel pictured on the facing page arranges the rainbow spectrum in a circle. It clearly shows the interrelationships of colors and illustrates a number of color principles.

Primary. Red, yellow, and blue are called *primary* colors. All other colors can be produced by various mixtures of these three. Conversely, no mixture of other colors will produce pure spectrum red, yellow, or blue. These three colors are spaced equally apart around the color wheel.

Complementary. Colors that face one another across the wheel—red and green, blue and orange, for example—are said to be complementary to one another. This means that if you were to mix paints of two complementary colors, they would neutralize, or complement, each other and make a shade of gray. Placing two complementary colors side by side, however, presents a strong contrast.

Harmonious. Colors that lie between any two primary colors are said to be harmonious with one another. This simply means that they are graduated mixtures of those two primary colors. For

example, the transition from yellow to red—through yellow orange, orange and red orange—is accomplished by gradually adding more red to yellow. The closer together two colors are in the spectrum, the more harmonious they are.

Warm versus cool. The color spectrum divides into two easily recognizable halves: warm colors and cool colors. The warm tones center around orange, the cool colors center around blue. The dividing line would be drawn between green and yellow green on one side and red and red violet on the other.

Color value—light to dark. Not only does the color wheel show relationships of one color to another, it also shows that a single color has a range of different values from light to dark. Each pure spectrum color in the wheel has the color name imprinted over it. Each of these pure colors becomes lighter in value toward the center of the wheel as it is diluted with more and more white. Toward the outside of the wheel, each color becomes darker in value with the addition of black.

Color principles in practice

Color is much more complex than the brief exposition above would indicate, but just that bit of basic information can help you plan a garden in which the colors will seem right.

Contrasts. Color contrasts can provide punctuation, focal points, relief from monotony, and even a sense of exhilaration in your garden. Such contrasts are produced by placing complementary colors (those that appear opposite one another on the color wheel) side by side in the garden. In most cases the contrasts will come from the flower colors. Notice, however, that the complement to red is green: brilliant red flowers

(Continued on page 18)

Contrast *is produced by combining complementary yellow calendulas with blue violet bachelor's buttons.*

Primary colors *—red (phlox) and yellow (rudbeckia)—make a dazzling combination with blue and pinkish white phlox.*

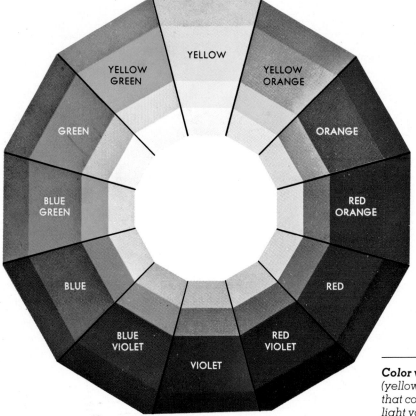

YELLOW

YELLOW GREEN

YELLOW ORANGE

GREEN

ORANGE

BLUE GREEN

RED ORANGE

BLUE

RED

BLUE VIOLET

RED VIOLET

VIOLET

Color wheel *shows primary colors (yellow, red, blue), transitional colors that connect them, and dark through light values of each color.*

...*Continued from page 16*

against a backdrop of green foliage provides as much of a contrast as yellow daylilies beside violet delphiniums. Any two, or all three, of the primary colors in combination also give a contrasting effect.

Contrasts are most effective when they're used as accents or foils to quieter, more harmonious color schemes (see "Harmonies," below). Used in excess, contrasts lose their impact and can even become disquieting. A mass of orange marigolds could be interestingly highlighted by a flash of blue delphiniums. Yet a planting that contained masses of both in equal amounts would be somehow displeasing to most viewers. Overwhelming, assertive contrast becomes boring.

Remember that contrasts don't occur only between colors at their full value. Cream and lavender, for example, have the same contrasting relationship as yellow and violet. The addition of white to the full colors has a modifying influence, but does not change the complementary relationships, as the inner bands of the color wheel show.

A third application of the contrast principle is the combination of contrasting colors and contrasting values. Full blue in combination with pale peach is just a variation on the blue and orange contrast. Pink geraniums against a green hedge is only a toned-down version of red geraniums against the same background.

Harmonies. Garden plantings composed of harmonious colors (those that lie between any two primary colors on the color wheel) are very pleasing to the eye. A planting of just warm or just cool colors can also be extremely satisfying. What such plantings tend to lack— especially if the colors are all about the same value—is zest. To bring them to life, they need some sort of contrast—contrast in values within the harmonious color group, or a burst of complementary color, or just white.

(Continued on page 20)

Pleasant grouping of cool colors features lavender Nepeta faassenii *spreading before blue* Nierembergia hippomanica violacea.

Warm color scheme of red, pink, orange, and yellow is highlighted by sharply contrasting drift of white; the flowers are snapdragons.

Marigolds, ranging from palest yellow to deepest orange and bronze tones, offer warm color harmonies.

Petunias illustrate agreeable combination of red and red violet that straddles the line between warm and cool colors.

Two values of one color are represented in this planting of red nicotiana and pink (red lightened by white) Cosmos.

...*Continued from page 18*

Gray. The great moderator of colors is gray. Usually thought of as a cool color, gray—in the form of gray-leafed plants—mingles comfortably with colors on the cool side of the color wheel. But the color gray results from the mixture of any two complementary colors (see page 16), so it can also be employed to tie together two otherwise contrasting colors. Imagine first a mass planting of yellow and violet violas, then envision those same colors surrounding a clump of silvery gray dusty miller. The contrast still exists, but softened or downgraded by the presence of the gray-leafed plant.

White. Any color's value decreases with the addition of white until the point is reached —represented by the center of the color wheel—where color is absent and only white is left. White flowers, then, can assort with all colors but in two different ways. With the lighter values of the various colors, white appears as harmonious; its absence of color appears closely related to the pale values around it. With colors at full and darker than full value, however, white stands out in sharp contrast.

Recalling that an overuse of contrasts can give an unsettling effect, white as a contrasting color should be used sparingly. Or, if white is to be the theme, then contrasting full-value colors should be employed with discretion. With lighter values, white can be used more lavishly to good effect.

All primary colors are present in Primula polyantha, *one of the few plants that embody all three primary colors. Edge is* Viola cornuta.

Dominant theme is warm colors of Nemesia strumosa *and Iceland poppy* (Papaver nudicaule). *White sweet alyssum gives contrast.*

White marguerites bring balance between contrasting orange lilies (they're bulbs) and blue bachelor's buttons. Design: R. David Adams.

Planting of coleus and impatiens shows strong contrast between red flowers and foliage and green foliage; white is accent.

Gray foliage of Centaurea cineraria moderates warm harmonies of calceolaria, Peruvian verbena, pelargonium, and scarlet sage.

Flower Garden Ideas **21**

Guide to color through the seasons

To plan effective combinations of garden color, you need to know what times of year your chosen plants will produce their colors. On these six pages are listed the most popular annuals and perennials according to their seasons of bloom and, for each plant, the flower colors it can offer.

Stately but graceful, tall bearded irises are a dominant presence in spring perennial garden.

Spring Annuals

Name	Red	Pink	Yellow	Orange	Blue	Purple	White	Multicolor	Green
Arctotis	●	●	●	●		●	●	●	
Bachelor's button	●	●			●		●		
Calendula			●	●					
California poppy	●	●	●	●			●		
Candytuft	●	●				●	●		
Cineraria	●	●			●	●	●	●	
Clarkia	●	●				●	●		
Dimorphotheca			●	●			●	●	
Fairy primrose	●	●				●	●		
Forget-me-not					●				
Iceland poppy	●	●	●	●			●		
Nasturtium	●		●	●			●		
Nemesia	●	●	●	●	●	●	●	●	
Nemophila					●		●		

Name	Red	Pink	Yellow	Orange	Blue	Purple	White	Multicolor	Green
Pansy	●		●	●	●	●	●	●	
Petunia	●	●	●	●	●	●	●	●	
Scarlet flax	●								
Schizanthus	●	●				●	●	●	
Shirley poppy	●	●		●			●	●	
Snapdragon	●	●	●	●			●		
Statice	●				●	●	●	●	
Stock	●	●				●	●		
Swan River daisy	●				●		●	●	
Sweet alyssum		●				●	●		
Sweet pea	●	●			●	●	●		
Sweet sultan	●		●			●	●		
Viola	●		●		●	●	●		

Spring Perennials

Name	Red	Pink	Yellow	Orange	Blue	Purple	White	Multicolor	Green
Acanthus mollis		●				●	●		
Alstroemeria	●	●	●	●		●	●	●	
Aquilegia	●		●		●	●	●	●	
Arctotis acaulis			●			●		●	
Aurinia saxatilis			●						
Bergenia	●	●				●	●		
Campanula		●			●	●	●		
Centranthus ruber	●	●							
Convallaria majalis							●		
Coreopsis	●		●	●					
Dicentra	●	●					●		
Dietes				●		●	●	●	
Digitalis		●	●			●	●	●	
Epimedium	●	●	●				●		
Euphorbia									●
Euryops		●							
Gazania	●	●	●	●			●	●	
Glechoma hederacea					●				
Helleborus						●	●	●	●
Hemerocallis	●	●	●	●		●	●	●	

Name	Red	Pink	Yellow	Orange	Blue	Purple	White	Multicolor	Green
Heuchera	●	●					●		●
Iberis sempervirens	●	●				●	●		
Iris	●	●	●	●	●	●	●	●	●
Kniphofia	●		●	●				●	
Lupinus	●	●	●	●	●	●	●	●	
Lychnis	●	●							
Osteospermum fruticosum						●	●	●	
Paeonia	●	●	●			●	●		
Papaver orientale	●	●		●			●		
Pelargonium	●	●		●			●	●	
Penstemon	●	●			●	●	●	●	
Phlox	●	●			●	●	●	●	
Polemonium						●	●		
Primula	●	●	●	●	●	●	●	●	
Trillium	●	●					●	●	
Trollius			●	●					
Viola	●	●	●	●	●	●	●		
Zantedeschia	●	●	●				●	●	

Summer Annuals

Name	Red	Pink	Yellow	Orange	Blue	Purple	White	Multicolor	Green
Ageratum		●			●	●	●		
Arctotis	●	●	●	●		●	●	●	
Baby's breath		●					●		
Bachelor's button	●	●			●		●		
Bedding begonia	●	●					●		
Bedding dahlia	●	●	●	●		●	●		
Bells-of-Ireland									●
Browallia					●	●	●		
Calceolaria	●		●					●	
Calendula				●	●				

Name	Red	Pink	Yellow	Orange	Blue	Purple	White	Multicolor	Green
California poppy	●	●	●	●			●		
Calliopsis	●		●	●		●		●	
Candytuft	●	●				●	●		
Celosia	●	●	●	●		●			
China aster	●	●			●	●	●		
Cineraria	●	●			●	●	●	●	
Clarkia	●	●				●	●		
Cleome		●				●			
Coleus	●	●	●	●		●		●	●
Cosmos	●	●	●	●		●	●	●	

(Continued on next page)

Name	Red	Pink	Yellow	Orange	Blue	Purple	White	Multicolor	Green
Forget-me-not					●				
Four o'clock	●	●	●	●			●	●	
Gaillardia	●		●	●				●	
Iceland Poppy	●	●	●	●			●		
Impatiens	●	●		●		●	●	●	
Lobelia	●				●	●	●		
Lupinus	●				●	●	●		
Lychnis	●	●			●	●	●		
Madagascar periwinkle	●	●					●	●	
Marigold	●		●	●			●	●	
Mignonette			●						●
Monkey flower	●		●					●	
Morning glory	●	●			●	●	●		
Nasturtium	●		●	●			●		
Nemesia	●	●	●	●	●	●	●		
Nemophila					●		●		
Nicotiana	●	●				●	●		●
Pansy	●		●	●	●	●	●	●	
Petunia	●	●	●	●	●	●	●	●	
Phlox	●	●	●			●	●		

Name	Red	Pink	Yellow	Orange	Blue	Purple	White	Multicolor	Green
Portulaca	●	●	●	●			●		
Scabiosa	●	●				●	●		
Scarlet flax	●								
Schizanthus	●	●				●	●	●	
Shirley poppy	●	●		●			●	●	
Snapdragon	●	●	●	●			●		
Snow-on-the-mountain							●	●	●
Statice	●		●	●	●		●	●	
Strawflower	●	●	●	●			●		
Summer chrysanthemum	●	●	●	●		●	●	●	
Sunflower	●		●	●					
Swan River daisy	●				●		●		
Sweet alyssum		●				●	●		
Sweet pea	●	●				●	●	●	
Sweet sultan	●		●			●	●		
Tithonia	●		●	●				●	
Verbena	●	●			●	●	●		
Viola	●		●		●	●	●		
Zinnia	●	●	●	●		●	●	●	●

Summer Perennials

Name	Red	Pink	Yellow	Orange	Blue	Purple	White	Multicolor	Green
Acanthus mollis		●				●	●		
Achillea	●	●	●				●		
Aconitum					●	●			
Agapanthus					●		●		
Alcea rosea	●	●	●	●		●	●		
Alstroemeria	●	●	●	●		●	●	●	
Anchusa azurea					●				
Anthemis			●	●			●		
Aquilegia	●		●		●	●	●	●	
Arctotis acaulis			●			●		●	
Artemisia			●				●		
Asclepias tuberosa	●		●	●					
Aster	●	●			●	●	●		
Astilbe	●	●					●		
Aurinia saxatilis			●						
Campanula		●			●	●	●		
Canna	●	●	●	●			●	●	
Centaurea cineraria			●			●			

Name	Red	Pink	Yellow	Orange	Blue	Purple	White	Multicolor	Green
Centranthus ruber	●	●							
Cerastium tomentosum							●		
Chrysanthemum	●	●	●	●		●	●	●	
Convolvulus mauritanicus					●				
Coreopsis	●		●	●					
Delphinium	●	●			●	●	●		
Dianthus	●	●	●			●	●		
Dicentra	●	●					●		
Dietes					●		●		
Digitalis		●	●			●	●	●	
Echinacea	●			●		●	●		
Echinops					●				
Erigeron		●				●	●		
Gaillardia grandiflora	●		●	●				●	
Gazania	●	●	●	●			●	●	
Geranium		●				●	●	●	
Geum	●		●	●					

...Summer perennials (cont'd.)

Name	Red	Pink	Yellow	Orange	Blue	Purple	White	Multicolor	Green
Glechoma hederacea					●				
Gypsophila paniculata							●		
Helenium	●		●	●				●	
Helianthus multiflorus			●						
Hemerocallis	●	●	●	●		●	●	●	
Heuchera	●	●				●			●
Hibiscus moscheutos	●	●					●	●	
Hosta					●	●	●		
Iberis sempervirens							●		
Iris	●	●	●	●	●	●	●	●	●
Kniphofia	●		●	●			●	●	
Lathyrus latifolius		●				●	●		
Liatris		●				●	●		
Limonium		●				●	●	●	
Linum				●	●		●	●	
Liriope						●	●		
Lobelia cardinalis	●								
Lupinus	●	●	●	●	●	●	●	●	
Lychnis	●	●					●		
Lythrum	●	●							
Mimulus	●	●	●				●	●	
Myosotis		●			●		●		
Nepeta faassenii					●	●	●		
Nierembergia					●	●	●	●	
Oenothera			●	●	●				

Name	Red	Pink	Yellow	Orange	Blue	Purple	White	Multicolor	Green
Ophiopogon						●	●		
Osteospermum						●	●	●	
Papaver orientale	●	●		●			●	●	
Pelargonium	●	●		●			●	●	
Penstemon	●	●	●		●	●	●		
Phlox	●	●				●	●	●	
Physostegia		●					●		
Platycodon		●				●	●		
Polemonium					●	●	●		
Primula	●	●	●	●	●	●	●	●	
Pulmonaria						●	●	●	
Rudbeckia	●		●	●				●	
Salvia					●	●			
Scabiosa		●			●	●	●		
Sedum	●	●	●				●		
Senecio cineraria		●							
Stachys						●			
Stokesia					●		●		
Thalictrum		●				●	●		
Trollius			●	●					
Veronica		●				●	●		
Verbena	●	●			●	●	●	●	
Viola	●	●	●	●	●	●	●	●	
Zantedeschia	●	●	●				●	●	

Ethereal white Phlox paniculata in a green setting gives feeling of coolness to a midsummer garden.

Autumn Annuals

Name	Red	Pink	Yellow	Orange	Blue	Purple	White	Multicolor	Green
Ageratum		●			●		●		
Baby's breath	●	●					●		
Bedding begonia	●	●					●		
Bedding dahlia	●	●	●	●		●	●		
Calceolaria	●		●					●	
Calendula			●	●					
Calliopsis	●		●	●		●		●	
Cosmos	●	●	●	●		●	●		
Flowering cabbage	●					●	●		●
Four o'clock	●	●	●			●	●		
Lobelia	●				●	●	●		
Marigold	●		●	●			●		
Morning glory	●	●			●	●	●	●	

Name	Red	Pink	Yellow	Orange	Blue	Purple	White	Multicolor	Green
Nasturtium	●		●	●			●		
Phlox	●	●	●			●	●		
Portulaca	●	●	●	●			●		
Salpiglossis	●	●	●	●		●		●	
Scabiosa	●	●				●	●		
Scarlet sage	●	●				●	●		
Summer chrysanthemum	●	●	●	●		●		●	
Sunflower	●		●	●					
Sweet alyssum		●				●	●		
Tithonia	●		●	●					
Verbena	●	●			●	●	●		
Zinnia	●	●	●	●		●	●	●	●

Autumn Perennials

Name	Red	Pink	Yellow	Orange	Blue	Purple	White	Multicolor	Green
Aconitum					●	●			
Anchusa azurea					●				
Anemone hybrida	●	●					●		
Anthemis tinctoria			●	●			●		
Aster	●	●			●	●	●		
Campanula					●	●	●		
Canna	●	●	●	●			●	●	
Chrysanthemum	●	●	●	●		●	●	●	
Convolvulus mauritanicus					●				
Coreopsis	●		●	●					
Delphinium	●	●	●		●	●	●		
Dianthus	●	●	●	●		●	●	●	
Dicentra eximia	●	●					●		
Dietes				●		●	●	●	
Digitalis		●	●			●	●	●	
Echinops					●				
Erigeron		●				●	●		
Gaillardia grandiflora	●		●					●	
Gazania	●	●	●	●		●	●	●	

Name	Red	Pink	Yellow	Orange	Blue	Purple	White	Multicolor	Green
Geranium		●			●	●	●		
Gypsophila paniculata							●		
Helenium	●		●	●				●	
Helianthus multiflorus			●						
Hemerocallis	●	●	●	●		●	●	●	
Hibiscus moscheutos	●	●					●	●	
Lathyrus latifolius		●				●	●		
Liatris		●				●	●		
Lythrum	●	●							
Osteospermum						●	●		
Rudbeckia	●		●	●				●	
Salvia					●	●			
Scabiosa		●			●	●	●		
Sedum	●	●	●				●		
Stokesia						●	●		
Verbena	●	●			●	●	●	●	

Decorative flowering cabbage will bring color to winter gardens in areas where winter is fairly mild.

Chrysanthemums are nearly synonymous with autumn. They come in all colors but blue, many flower styles.

Winter Annuals

Name	Red	Pink	Yellow	Orange	Blue	Purple	White	Multicolor	Green
Calendula			●	●					
Cineraria	●	●			●	●	●	●	
Dimorphotheca			●	●			●	●	
Fairy primrose	●	●				●	●		
Flowering cabbage	●					●	●	●	●
Iceland poppy			●	●	●		●		

Name	Red	Pink	Yellow	Orange	Blue	Purple	White	Multicolor	Green
Pansy	●		●	●	●	●	●	●	
Snapdragon	●	●	●	●			●		
Stock	●	●				●	●		
Sweet alyssum		●				●	●		
Sweet pea	●	●				●	●	●	
Viola	●		●		●	●	●		

Winter Perennials

Name	Red	Pink	Yellow	Orange	Blue	Purple	White	Multicolor	Green
Bergenia crassifolia		●				●			
Euryops			●						
Helleborus		●				●	●	●	●

Name	Red	Pink	Yellow	Orange	Blue	Purple	White	Multicolor	Green
Osteospermum						●	●	●	
Primula	●	●	●	●	●	●	●	●	

Exuberant living bouquet combines annuals (lobelia, verbena, dianthus, nemesia) and perennials (Lychnis viscaria, Chrysanthemum frutescens). *Design: R. David Adams.*

Containers offer living bouquets

Splashy container plantings are simple to create and virtually foolproof as long as you follow some simple guidelines. Select plants that will grow well in your climate and keep them watered, fed, and groomed routinely so they will bloom heavily for a long period. Annuals form the backbone of container plantings, but some perennials also grow well in containers.

As soon as young plants are available in your local nursery or garden center and the danger of serious frost is past, you can start to assemble these living bouquets. First, you will need a large container, at least 18 inches wide and as deep. This will give plants ample root space and will be in scale with the luxuriant plant growth. Suitable containers include terra cotta pots, paper pulp pots, wooden tubs, half barrels, or box planters. Whichever you choose, fill it with a container planting mixture described on page 13.

To achieve a bountifully over-flowing appearance, space plants about four to six inches apart, much closer than you would plant them in the garden. Forcing the plants to compete for space makes them grow up and out, intermingling much as they would as cut flowers in a vase.

Give plants a continuous supply of moisture and ample fertilizer to get them off to a good start and to keep them going. Never let the soil dry out. Slow-

(Continued on page 30)

Trailing bouquets can be effective. In flower are yellow calceolaria, white browallia, and pink Pelargonium peltatum. Design: Egon Molbak.

Overflowing entry bouquets mix together schizanthus, lobelia, and Chrysanthemum frutescens. Large leaves are fig. Design: R. David Adams.

… living bouquets

release fertilizers that release nutrients to the plants each time the container is watered are a good choice for keeping these plantings growing vigorously. If you feel plants aren't getting enough nutrients from the slow-release fertilizer, you can supplement it with occasional applications of a liquid fertilizer. Or, you can depend entirely on liquid fertilizer applications every 7 to 10 days.

Grooming plants is especially important, and not just to maintain neatness. Many of these plants will divert their energies from blooming to setting seed if you leave spent flowers on the plants. Remove the faded flowers each day to help encourage continual flower production. Pinch back or cut back any plants that become unattractively leggy. This will encourage them to branch more and ultimately produce more flowers.

Two primary colors are skillfully combined in separate pots of red and yellow celosia backed by container of red and yellow marigolds.

Scarlet sage needs no accompaniment to create an eye-catching splash of container color.

Harmonious mixed colors of dianthus are unified by the single flower shape. White flowers provide accent.

Just green and white: Container of daisy-flowered Chrysanthemum frutescens is framed by Acanthus mollis.

Potted petunias, here in red and yellow, provide bountiful summertime displays in all parts of the country.

Flower Garden Ideas **31**

Patriotic display contains mix of naturalized wildflowers; red Shirley poppy (Papaver rhoeas), white Queen Anne's lace, blue bachelor's buttons.

A natural look with wildflowers

The carefree charm of an open flowering field can be brought to your garden by planting wild-flowers. Wildflower seeds are sold in packets in many nurseries and are available through several mail-order seed companies. The exact wildflowers included in mixtures will vary in different parts of the country.

Ideally you want to sow the seeds just before the normal rainy season so that natural rainfall will take care of much of the plants' water needs. In areas of the country where the ground is frozen in winter or covered with snow, you sow wildflower seeds as soon as the danger of the last hard frost is over. These wildflowers will bloom mostly in spring and summer.

In winter rainfall areas of the western states where the ground does not freeze during winter, sow seeds in fall for a floral display in later winter, spring, to early summer.

The time of year for preparing the soil and sowing seeds depends on your local climate, but the procedures are the same wherever you live. First, clear and till the soil in the area you intend to plant. Use a rotary tiller to prepare a large area of soil; hand dig smaller areas. After turning the soil, rake it to remove rocks, to break up large dirt clods, and to smooth and level the soil. Then the soil's ready for planting.

Carefully scatter the seeds onto the soil by hand or tap them out of the seed packet. For easier sowing and a more even distribution of seeds, you can mix the seeds with four parts sand and scatter the mixture over the soil.

If you have a large area to plant, simply broadcast the seeds. Place the seed/sand mixture in a bowl and, walking backward, fling handfuls of the mixture in broad arcs over the prepared soil. For a more even distribution, divide the seed/sand mixture into two equal parts; broadcast one part over the whole area, then broadcast the second part over the same area but walk at a right angle to your first direction. If broadcasting seems too chancy, you may be able to rent or buy a crank-operated seeder that you hang from your neck. Then you just crank out the seeds as you walk. Smaller areas may also be seeded by the broadcast method, but do it a bit more carefully.

After you have seeded the ground, water it thoroughly with a fine spray. The fine spray is important to get the seeds into good contact with the soil without washing them out. Keep soil moist until seeds sprout.

Waves of orange *California poppies (Eschscholzia californica) are punctuated by spots of red flax (Linum grandiflorum 'Rubrum').*

Flamboyant color *and masses of it are the midspring contribution of Clarkia amoena to wildflower plantings.*

Low-growing *baby blue eyes (Nemophila menziesii) will bring early spring sparkle to moist areas of the garden.*

Flower Garden Ideas **33**

Grandeur with grand scale

Grand borders of perennials and annuals are impressive. But even if you don't have the space and time to grow such large-scale plantings as these, you can still make note of how plants of various colors, shapes, and sizes are used together in interesting ways.

Classic perennial border backed by hedge includes tall yellow verbascum, yellow yarrow, lavender catmint.

Wide sweeping border combines perennials of different heights and shapes. In the foreground are baby's breath, Shasta daisies, sedum.

Massed annuals can imitate a perennial border. Included here are cosmos, petunias, Swan River daisy, sweet alyssum, zinnias.

Foliage textures and colors are important as floral display in this perennial border. Foxglove, red hot poker, veronica, Maltese cross are among the plants in flower; foliage plants will bloom later.

Narrow bed combines plants with foliage masses of similar height. In the foreground baby's breath, coreopsis, artemisia, and yarrow grow.

Annuals & perennials: Perfect partners

Capitalizing on color, these gardens demonstrate the effectiveness of combining, in the same planting, annuals, perennials, and (in two gardens) flowering shrubs. With perennials (and shrubs) as garden backbones, annuals fill in with drifts of color during the growing season.

Lavish display results from carefree association of roses with various annuals and perennials.

Elevated view (above) of garden at left shows riotous mix of colors from annuals, perennials, lilies, roses. Dense spikes of flowers are lupines.

Annual snapdragons (pink, red tones) and calendulas (yellow, orange) infiltrate plantings of irises and blue marguerites (Felicia amelloides).

...more combinations

Narrow border uses perennial delphiniums and Shasta daisies for height, annual petunias and nemesia for low color. Design: R. David Adams.

Yellow yarrow, white Shasta daisies, and blue salvia dominate seaside garden. Orange marigolds (center) give spark of contrast.

High summer bounty stems from annual marigolds, zinnias, and violas in foreground, perennial Rudbeckia hirta at back.

Early spring *brings forth annual violas and Johnny-jump-ups, perennial white candytuft (Iberis), plus fairy and polyanthus primroses.*

Flower Garden Ideas **39**

If fragrance is your fancy

Beauty is not just in color and form—many flowers include fragrance as a part of their allure. Some release perfume throughout the garden, others demurely offer it to you at nose-distance. By virtue of their fragrance and the charm this adds in the home, many also are favored as cut flowers.

Sweet and spicy is the fragrance that emanates from stock. Flowers come in soft shades of white, cream, and pink through purple.

Honey-scented sweet alyssum is old-fashioned favorite for edging and carpet planting. Plants reseed themselves freely, year after year.

Aptly-named sweet pea comes in great range of colors from brilliant through soft tones; it is one of the best flowers for cutting.

Pleasantly fragrant nasturtiums
flourish, may even run rampant,
where summers and winters
are mild.

Cut-flower candidates

If people had limitless time to spend in the garden, cut flowers might have less appeal. But when garden time is dessert to the meat-and-potatoes of daily life, cut blossoms in a vase increase the amount of time each particular flower can be savored.

Intricately patterned blossoms of salpiglossis attract close-up viewing; colors include warm shades, pink, purple.

Prolific coral bells (Heuchera) provide enough bloom for lavish garden display as well as for cut flowers.

Delicate-appearing alstroemeria give long life as cut flowers. Other colors are white, cream, yellow, orange, red.

...for vases & arrangements

Sunny calendulas *provide ongoing supply of blooms for cutting. These annual plants live longer where winters are mild.*

Shaggy annual aster (Callistephus chinensis) *gives summer bloom in shades of pink, red, white, and magenta through purple to violet.*

Iceland poppies (Papaver nudicaule) come into their prime in late winter/ early spring where winter is mild. Sear stem ends after cutting.

Sparklingly fresh Shasta daisies (Chrysanthemum maximum) produce plenty of long-stemmed blooms for garden and house.

Delicate-looking flowers and feathery foliage belie tough constitution of annual cosmos; season is summer and fall.

For everlasting bouquets

You can achieve the illusion of eternal spring (or summer) by growing annuals and perennials that retain their forms and colors after being cut and dried. A bouquet of such flowers can give pleasant reminders of the growing season's warmth and bounty throughout the year.

Annual statice (Limonium sinuatum) *and its perennial counterparts give pink to purple, paper-textured flowers.*

Dry-looking *even when fresh, straw-flower (Helichrysum bracteatum) will last for years in dried arrangements.*

Haze of bloom *nearly obscures plant of perennial baby's breath (Gypsophila paniculata), a good filler for dried bouquets.*

Either fresh or dried, *bells-of-Ireland (Moluccella laevis) will provide an unusual green accent to bouquets.*

Perpetual favorites where winters are cold

In the world of plants there are those that revel in winter cold versus those that abhor it. Not all cold-winter plants need arctic chill in order to perform, but they do require winter temperatures below freezing to develop full growth and beauty.

Spectacular is the word for Oriental poppy (Papaver orientale), whether in typical red orange or in pastel shades.

Long-spurred columbines (Aquilegia hybrids) bring a variety of colors in gracefully airborne flowers to lightly shaded gardens.

Living valentines—spring blossoms of common bleeding heart (Dicentra spectabilis)—enhance moist, shaded gardens.

Opulent peonies (Paeonia officinalis hybrids) have long been cherished for beautiful, dependable performance.

These thrive with little water

Plants suffer from water limitation in many situations: actual desert conditions, no rainfall during the growing season, soil that dries out rapidly, a gardener disinclined or unable to water. In such instances, it's best to choose drought-resistant plants that can thrive despite limited water.

Abundance of golden wheels typifies perennial coreopsis that blooms through summer with little attention.

Satin-textured blossoms of Portulaca grandiflora resemble small roses and come steadily with minimum water.

Red valerian (Centranthus ruber) may be rosy red, dusty pink, or white; all thrive with minimal care.

Yarrows (Achillea species) are good choices for color in borders that contain plants, such as iris, that need little water in summer.

For some, the wetter the better

A limited number of popular garden annuals and perennials thrive on an abundance of water. Some of these will grow in boggy soil that is too saturated for most flowering plants; others simply need soil that is constantly moist but neither saturated nor ever dry.

Feathery plumes of astilbe flowers are spring and summer dividends; plants have handsome foliage.

Adaptable calla lilies (Zantedeschia) *bring chiseled elegance in white, yellow, pink, or red to average and marshy soils.*

Sumptuous Japanese irises *raise plate-size blossoms over fountains of graceful foliage in late spring.*

Spritely monkey flower (Mimulus) *will light up shaded, damp areas frequented by ferns.*

Stunning sun worshipers

Light is vital to the growth of all plants. For a great many popular annuals and perennials, this translates into lots of direct sunlight. Given their individual soil and water requirements plus the right amount of sunlight, these plants will return that light as bountiful, brilliant color.

'Blue Bedder' penstemon offers strikingly brilliant blue flowers on spreading plants that are good along borders and pathways.

Zinnias offer a wide range of bright colors in a variety of sizes to suit many garden needs.

Warmth of summer *is captured in* Rudbeckia hirta—*black-eyed Susan or coneflower.*

Cup flowers (Nierembergia) *give summerlong display of refreshingly cool blue or white blossoms.*

Solid colors *or gaily striped flowers are possible with afternoon-blooming four o'clocks* (Mirabilis jalapa).

Flashy flowers and flamboyant foliage of New Guinea hybrid impatiens will perk up a shaded garden.

Brighten up your garden's shadows

Shade and shadow may suggest quiet and restraint, but many of the shade-preferring plants are anything but restrained—shouting out at you, instead, with vivid color. A cool atmosphere is almost always the basic requirement among the shade lovers, for some will grow in full-sun locations where summers are cool and light intensity is low.

Attractive flower clusters are a bonus with bergenia's always-handsome clumps of broad, polished leaves.

Favorite foliage plants especially in colder regions, hostas come in a wide range of colors, patterns, and sizes.

Traffic-stopping cinerarias (Senecio hybridus) encompass colors from red through blue, plus white and pink.

Blue stars furnish late spring/early summer decoration to vigorous Campanula poscharskyana.

Low to the ground — but lovely

A number of favorite annuals and perennials put on their displays only slightly above ground level. These plants are often used as edging for a paved or gravel path. And they also can be spread out like rugs: in drifts of one plant for solid color, or several plants mixed together like patterns in fine Oriental carpets.

Basket of gold (Aurinia saxatile) *will overflow with brilliance along pathways and in foreground plantings.*

Gazanias offer a broad range of colors and patterns, have a long flowering season, and need minimal care.

Harmonious *foreground association features blue* Convolvulus mauritanicus *and dark-centered* Osteospermum fruticosum.

Versatile Verbena hybrida *will serve as edging plant or ground cover; comes in wide range of bright colors.*

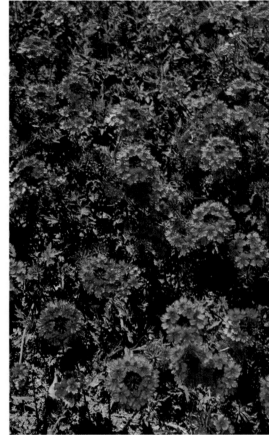

Widely adapted *snow-in-summer* (Cerastium tomentosum) *gives cool silvery foliage all year, carpet of snowy blossoms in summer.*

Front-row favorites

The category of "border plants" contains some of the most useful annuals and perennials. They serve, of course, as foregrounds to taller plants, but they often are just the right choices where planting areas are small with no room for background plants. Many also are popular for containers.

Dwarf bedding dahlias, miniature bushy versions of their spectacular 6-foot kin, come in all colors but blue.

Annual phlox brings the look of its perennial relatives to small mounding plants (6–18 inches) with long bloom season.

Ageratum or floss flower has overall look of softness; colors include pink, white, and blue and lavender shades.

Pansies come in a seemingly infinite range of colors and patterns; most flowers combine two or more shades.

High-rise color

Flowers lifted to eye-height (or above) add visual punctuation to a garden the same way skyscrapers do in a city skyline. Some of these flowers are unabashedly dramatic, others are more quietly interesting. But even with those differences aside, all will be noticed.

Hollyhock spires (Alcea rosea) elevate garden color as high as 9 feet in some strains; flowers come in pastel to bright colors.

Mammoth annual sunflowers growing up to 10 feet offer visual drama, plus a crop of edible seeds after blooms are gone.

Foxgloves (Digitalis) stand 2–8 feet tall and bloom in soft colors. They come as perennials, biennials, even annuals.

Vigorous Physostegia virginiana also comes in pink shades; gives plenty of summer bloom with little special care.

Aristocrats for background, delphiniums, in favored climates, well repay the extra care they need.

Annuals & Perennials, A to Z

The following pages will acquaint you with proven, popular annuals and perennials, as well as a number of fine plants deserving wider appreciation. To introduce each plant we give its botanical name and common name (if it has one), then its hardiness to low winter temperature and any other climate restriction. A profile of the plant follows the introduction. It includes a description of foliage, flowers, and plant habit; mention of the plant's strong or weak points; and cultural advice, such as soil and exposure preference, water needs, dividing or propagating suggestions (for perennials), and any special pest or disease cautions. From these concise profiles you'll be able to evaluate each plant's potential usefulness in your own garden.

Riotous display of annuals and perennials surrounds this well-tended, sheltered garden. Much of color impact stems from contrasts.

Acanthus mollis

Bear's breech or breeches
Perennial, hardy to about 5°F/−15°C
Pictured on page 31

When not in bloom, acanthus clumps might be mistaken for rhubarb. The large, lobed to deeply cut 2-foot leaves are at the ends of long, thick leaf stalks that arise directly from the ground. The flowering spikes that appear in late spring and early summer look almost like foxgloves, or even snapdragons, with their white to rosy lilac blossoms hooded by spiny green bracts.

Except in hot-summer areas of the West and Southwest, acanthus will grow in full sun. Good, well-drained soil and regular watering are preferable, but plants can withstand some drought.

Clumps may need dividing after about 5 years. Do this in early spring where winters are freezing, in midautumn through late winter elsewhere. Caution: New plants can sprout and spread from any cut portion of root left in the ground. Don't divide the plants too often or cultivate around the roots.

Achillea

Yarrow
Perennial, hardy to −30°F/−34°C
Pictured on pages 34, 35, 38, 51

Yarrow may bring to mind a plant with flat clusters of yellow flowers on tall stems. But there are others with shorter or spreading growth and white, cream, pink, and red flowers.

There are several low-growing yarrows. *A. ageratifolia* (Greek yarrow) forms spreading mats of toothed silver gray leaves; it bears 1-inch clusters of white flowers on stems to 10 inches high. *A. clavennae* (*A. argentea*, Silvery yarrow) is of similar size and height, with silver gray leaves and pale cream flowers. *A. taygetea* grows to 18 inches with feather-cut, 4-inch, gray green leaves and bright sulfur yellow flowers. *A. tomentosa* (Woolly yarrow) forms mats of dark green fernlike leaves and flower stems 10 inches tall.

In the medium height range, *A. ptarmica* reaches about 2 feet tall bearing narrow green leaves and white flowers. *A. millefolium* has finely cut green to gray green leaves and white flowers; its varieties include several red-flowered kinds.

The tallest yarrows, from 3 to 5 feet, are forms or hybrids of *A. filipendulina* (Fernleaf yarrow), characterized by finely cut green leaves and yellow flowers.

Summer is peak yarrow season. Give plants full sun, reasonably good well-drained soil, and regular watering. Established clumps will tolerate quite a bit of drought. After bloom, cut spent stalks down to the base. Divide old clumps in spring.

Aconite. See **Aconitum**.

Aconitum

Monkshood, Aconite
Perennial, hardy to −30°F/−34°C; not for mild-winter/hot-summer climates

This unusual beauty carries a warning — all parts of the plant are very poisonous. Clumps of dark green, celerylike foliage grow from tuberous roots. In late summer or early autumn, flowering spikes shoot up as high as 8 feet. (Most kinds are 2–5 feet tall.) The dark blue to purple flowers have an unusual hooded shape and are carried close to the stem, giving an effect similar to delphinium.

The key to success is good, moist soil. Grow plants in sun or light shade. Clumps need dividing every 2–3 years. Do this in autumn (carefully mulching transplants during winter in coldest regions), winter, or earliest spring. Plants are completely dormant during winter.

African daisy. See **Arctotis, Dimorphotheca, Osteospermum**.

Agapanthus

Lily-of-the-Nile
Perennial, hardy to about 10°F/−12°C

These handsome plants might be grown just for their clumps of green, strap-shaped leaves were it not for their magnificent flowers: clusters of blue or white tubular blossoms topping slender stalks. Available kinds range in height from 1 to 5 feet.

Agapanthus needs well-drained

soil and, for best performance, regular watering. Clumps should be divided infrequently, perhaps every 6 years. The best time is late winter or early spring. In climates too cold for winter survival outdoors, grow them in large containers. Move them indoors in autumn to a cool spot and water sparingly until you take them outside in spring.

Ageratum houstonianum

Floss flower
Annual
Pictured on page 61

From early summer until frost, much-favored ageratum yields densely clustered tiny flowers in shades of lavender blue, pinkish lavender, or white. Spade-shaped leaves are light to medium green and hairy. In flower, these plants give an overall impression of softness. Smallest kinds may grow no more than 6 inches high; the largest may reach 2 feet. Many grow in the 9–18-inch range.

Give ageratum well-prepared soil and regular watering. Where summers are hot and dry, plants prefer light shade all day or morning sun only. Elsewhere, full sun is best. For mass effect, set smaller kinds about 9 inches apart, taller ones 12–18 inches apart. In mild-winter areas of the West and Southwest, set out plants in late summer for autumn and winter bloom.

Alcea rosea (Althaea rosea)

Hollyhock
Biennial or short-lived perennial, hardy to −35°F/−37°C
Pictured on page 62

Few plants suggest an old-fashioned garden as much as hollyhocks. Typically, they have saucer-shaped flowers about 4 inches wide on towering flower spikes 8 to 9 feet tall. Originally hollyhocks were biennials, but plant breeders have developed annual and perennial strains. In addition, you can choose some as short as 2 feet or a more moderate 5–6 feet. Summer flowers may be single, semi-double, or double, in yellow, cream, white, pink, rose, apricot, bronze red, maroon, and purple.

Leaves are large, rounded to somewhat lobed, and rough-hairy, on the ends of slender leaf stalks. Plants grow as a mound of foliage until flower spikes begin to elongate. Each plant may bear several flowering spikes.

Hollyhocks appreciate well-prepared soil and regular watering. Rust can plague their foliage, so choose rust-resistant strains. Remove and destroy any blighted leaves, or use one of the controls mentioned on page 15.

Alstroemeria

Peruvian lily
Perennial, hardy to 5°F/−15°C
Pictured on page 43

If you can imagine a lilylike plant bearing the flowers of a deciduous azalea, you have a picture of alstroemeria. Plants form spreading clumps of upright, leafy stems 2–5 feet tall. Atop them are loose clusters of trumpet-shaped flowers in white, cream, yellow, orange, pink, lilac, and red, often streaked or spotted with darker colors. The garden effect is informal and airy.

Alstroemerias bloom in summer, then gradually go into dormancy. Water plants regularly while they are growing and flowering. After bloom, they need little moisture. Grow them in part shade where summers are hot and dry, elsewhere in full sun.

Once established, alstroemerias need no digging and dividing. To limit the spread of plants from self-sown seeds, remove spent flower clusters.

Alum root. See **Heuchera**.

Amethyst flower. See **Browallia**.

Anchusa

Annual. Perennial, hardy to −30°F/−34°C

True blue, from light to dark, is anchusa's trademark. All look like their near relative, forget-me-not (*Myosotis*), but are larger and showier. Summer flowers (continuing into autumn) occur in large, branched clusters held above the foliage.

A. capensis (Cape or Summer forget-me-not) is an annual, to about 18 inches high with narrow, hairy,

5-inch leaves. Flowers open in many-branched clusters. Several named forms vary in height or color; there is also a white form.

A. azurea (A. italica) is perennial. Clumps of hairy, lance-shaped leaves to 1 foot long send up flowering spikes from 2 to 5 feet high, depending on variety.

Anchusas prefer full sun and good, well-drained soil with only moderate watering. Set out new plants at the start of the growing season.

Anemone hybrida

Anemone

Japanese anemone
Perennial, hardy to −20°F/−29°C

Japanese anemones, *A. hybrida* (sometimes sold as *A. japonica* or *A. hupehensis japonica*), are a bit slow to become established, but once they've settled in they can remain undisturbed for years. Dark green leaves with 3–5 serrated lobes grow in clumps. From these, in earliest autumn, arise slim branching stems 2–4 feet tall, bearing single, semi-double, or nearly double 2–3 inch-wide pink or white flowers.

The grape-leaved anemone, *A. tomentosa* (usually sold as *A. vitifolia* or *A. vitifolia* 'Robustissima'), is similar to Japanese anemones, but its pink flowers begin in late summer. It tends to spread more rapidly and to survive somewhat lower winter temperatures.

Both Japanese and grape-leaved anemones prefer good, well-drained soil and regular watering. In most areas give them light shade or filtered sunlight; where summers are cool they'll take full sun. Plantings really never need dividing.

Angel's hair. See **Artemisia**.

Anthemis tinctoria

Golden marguerite
Perennial, hardy to −30°F/−34°C; not suited to Gulf coast and Florida

Aromatic, finely cut leaves, densely clothe these mounded plants that grow 2–3 feet high and wide. Typical daisy flowers, to 2 inches across, cover plants in summer and early autumn. Flowers are yellow, gold, lemon, or white and yellow.

Anthemis is virtually trouble-free. It needs full sun, well-drained soil and a moderate amount of water. Plants bloom heavily and should be cut back after flowering. Start new plants from spring cuttings or by dividing clumps in autumn or spring.

Antirrhinum majus

Snapdragon
Annual
Pictured on pages 18, 37

Favored by many generations of gardeners for their vertical accents of bright colors, snapdragons also have been favorites of children because of their unique, lobed and hooded flowers that snap open like jaws when squeezed on the sides. Plant breeders have modified traditional snapdragons in several ways. Now you can get strains that are dwarf (to 8 inches), intermediate (20 to 30 inches), and tall (to 36 inches). And in some cases the "snap" has been taken away: there are strains with double flowers, and strains with flowers that are bell shaped or even double-bell shaped (azalea-flowered). These "snaplessdragons" also come in dwarf to tall sizes.

On all types, blooms are carried directly on upright flower spikes, on which flowers at the bottom bloom first. Modern snapdragons — available in every color but blue — make excellent cut flowers.

Plant in good, well-drained soil and water regularly. In mild-winter areas, snapdragons will bloom in winter and early spring if you set them out in early autumn. Where winters are colder, set out plants in early spring for late spring and summer flowers. Rust is this plant's worst enemy, but there are rust-resistant strains. Should rust develop, use a control suggested on page 15, and avoid overhead watering.

Aquilegia

Columbine
Perennial, hardy to −40°F/−40°C; not suited to Gulf coast, Florida
Pictured on page 48

This entire plant appears delicate and graceful — from the gray green, maidenhair-fernlike foliage to the slender branching stems that carry flowers seemingly poised for flight.

Each blossom consists of 5 inner petals that form a loose cup, 5 long pointed petals that form a sort of saucer for the cup, and 5 slender spurs that project backward from the saucer petals. Short-spurred and double-flowered sorts are also sold. Colors range from pure white through yellow, pink, red, purple, and lavender. Flowers may consist of two colors, with the cup petals usually lighter than the rest.

Filtered sunlight or light shade is usually best, though columbines can take full sun where summers are cool. Give them well-drained soil and regular watering. Aphids, spider mites, and leaf miners are possible pests; see page 15 for controls. Columbines are not long-lived perennials — about 3–4 years for an individual plant. You can dig and divide old clumps, but more certain success comes from new plants.

Arctotis

African daisy
Perennial, hardy to 10°F/−12°C

Both of the commonly sold kinds of perennial arctotis have 3-inch daisy-like flowers and gray green, hairy, somewhat lobed leaves. *A. acaulis* has yellow blossoms with black purple centers; flowers come on 6-inch stalks above clumps of foliage. Other plants, sold simply as Arctotis hybrids, form lax, spreading clumps to 18 inches high; flowers come in a variety of colors — white, cream, yellow, orange, red, pink, purple — usually with nearly black center surrounded by a dark ring. Bloom season is spring and early summer.

Full sun and well-drained soil are needed. Give plants regular watering while they're actively growing and flowering; otherwise, they get along with little. You can increase *A. acaulis* by digging and separating clumps. The Arctotis hybrids, propagated best from cuttings in spring,

are not long-lived, so you may want to take cuttings every year or two.

Artemisia

Wormwood
Perennial, hardy to −30°F/−34°C
Pictured on page 35

With one exception, artemisias are grown for their foliage beauty: silvery gray, often finely cut, and feathery. These gray-leafed sorts are good moderators among brightly colored flowers, and harmonizers in pastel color schemes. Their general effect is delicate rather than assertive. *A. lactiflora* (White mugwort) is the exception and is grown for its flowers: upright 4-foot stems topped by loose plumes of small creamy blossoms. Coarsely divided leaves are dark green.

Gray-leafed sorts are many. *A. frigida*, with finely cut, nearly white foliage on spreading plants, grows to 1½ feet tall. *A. ludoviciana albula* (*A. albula*), a bushy silver gray mound to 3 feet high, has lobed and unlobed leaves. *A. schmidtiana* (Angel's hair) makes a 2-foot-high mound of feathery, silvery foliage; its variety 'Silver Mound' is at most only half that size. *A. stellerana* (Beach wormwood, Old woman, Dusty miller) forms spreading clumps, to 2 feet high, of lobed gray white leaves.

Artemisias need full sun and well-drained soil, with only moderate watering. Removing flowering stems after bloom helps to keep them compact, so does occasional cutting back. After several years, plants may need dividing — in autumn or early spring.

Asclepias tuberosa

Butterfly weed
Perennial, hardy to −30°F/−34°C

With its brilliant orange flowers attracting butterflies, this "weed" is the very essence of summer. Each spring, many stems grow from a dormant root, reaching 2–3 feet high by the time bloom begins in midsummer. Individual flowers are small but grouped together in broad, flattened clusters atop each stem. Lance-shaped leaves to 4 inches long grow along the stems from ground level to the base of bloom clusters.

The tap-rooted plants prefer a deep, light soil and little to (at most)

Asclepias

moderate watering: roots may rot in heavy, damp soil. Clumps will increase in size as years go by, but can remain in the same place indefinitely. If you want additional plants, raise them from seed or take root cuttings of older plant in early spring.

Aster

Perennial, hardy to about −25°F/−32°C; not suited to Gulf coast and Florida

Numerous species and many hybrids comprise the perennial asters. The most familiar are known as Michaelmas daisies. Mostly sold are hybrids ranging in height from about 12 inches to over 4 feet. Plants form clumps of narrow leaves and send up branching spikes of typical daisy flowers, single to nearly double and generally 1–2 inches across. Shorter hybrids form almost solid mounds of color; tall ones are more open and graceful but often need staking. Colors include shades of lavender and pink—light to dark—plus white and red purples. Typical bloom season is midsummer into autumn.

Perennial asters are not fussy about soil, but they need full sun and regular watering. Mildew is one problem they may develop. They perform best with frequent dividing, so dig clumps about every other year. Do this in early spring where winters are cold, in autumn or spring in milder regions.

Astilbe

False spiraea, Meadow sweet
Perennial, hardy to −25°F/−32°C
Pictured on page 52

Commonly sold astilbe hybrids cover the range from 1½-foot shorties to back-of-the-border 6-footers. All possess the same beauty: neat clumps of compound, toothed, almost fernlike leaves above which project showy, featherlike plumes of individually tiny flowers. Colors include white, all shades of pink, red, and purplish magenta. Bloom season is summer.

Moist soil (but not boggy) is the key to success. Give astilbes a good soil with plenty of organic matter and regular watering. They will thrive at pool and pond margins if soil isn't saturated. All grow in full sun, provided moisture is available; but filtered sunlight or part shade is just as satisfactory – and necessary in hot-summer regions. Plant in autumn or spring. When bloom production declines (in 4–5 years), divide old clumps in spring.

Aurinia saxatilis

Basket-of-gold
Perennial, hardy to −35°F/−37°C
Pictured on page 58

Once called *Alyssum saxatile*, this plant is widely used for borders, foregrounds, small-scale ground cover, and rock gardens. Plants are low (to about 12 inches) and mounding-spreading, with narrow, gray to gray green leaves. Flowers appear in spring and early summer. They're individually small but grouped in rounded 1-inch clusters that cover the plant with vivid yellow. Several named varieties offer variations on this basic theme. For pale yellow flowers there are 'Citrina' ('Lutea') and 'Silver Queen.' 'Compacta' is a shorter, more dense plant; 'Flore Pleno' has double flowers.

Well-drained soil, full sun to light shade, and moderate watering are the basic requirements. Set out young plants in early spring. After bloom, shear off the old flower heads.

B

Baby blue eyes. See **Nemophila.**

Baby's breath. See **Gypsophila.**

Bachelor's button. See **Centaurea.**

Balloon Flower. See **Platycodon.**

Balsam. See **Impatiens.**

Basket-of-gold. See **Aurinia.**

Beach wormwood. See **Artemisia.**

Beard tongue. See **Penstemon.**

Bear's breeches. See **Acanthus.**

Bedding begonia. See **Begonia.**

Bedding dahlia. See **Dahlia.**

Begonia semperflorens-cultorum

Bedding begonia, Wax begonia
Perennial, hardy to about 10°F/ −12°C; grown as annual in cold-winter climates

A first-rate plant for borders, low mass-plantings, and containers, this begonia is attractive in or out of bloom. Depending on variety or strain, plants grow from 6 inches to 18 inches high and are compact and bushy. Glossy leaves are rounded, are up to 2½ inches across, and may be green, bronzy green, or bronze red. Flowers—either single or double —may be white, pink, or red. Flowers are usually about an inch wide, but there are strains with blooms to 3 inches across. The main bloom season is summer and early autumn, but where plants are perennial they can bloom all year.

Their requirements are simple: regular garden soil and routine watering. Set them out in spring in full sun where summers are cool, filtered sunlight or part shade elsewhere.

Bellflower. See **Campanula.**

Bells-of-Ireland. See **Moluccella.**

Bergenia

Perennial, hardy to −30°F/−34°C
Pictured on page 56

Even if bergenias never flowered, they would be worth planting for their handsome foliage. Individual leaves are oval to nearly round, leathery, deeply veined, and up to a foot long on equally long leaf stalks. The plant is a loose clump of these leaves. In established plants, the foliage may reach 1½ feet high. Bell-shaped flowers in spikes appear in winter, spring, or early summer.

Winter-blooming *B. crassifolia* is most commonly grown; flowers are rose pink to purplish pink. *B. cordifolia* has a pinkish spring bloom partly hidden in leaves; *B. ciliata* has white, pink, or purplish flowers in late spring through early summer.

Bergenias will grow under the most trying conditions, such as dry shade and poor soil, but they flourish in good soil with regular watering. Give full sun where summers are cool, filtered sun to part shade elsewhere. Divide in late winter or early spring.

Bishop's hat. See **Epimedium.**

Black-eyed Susan. See **Rudbeckia.**

Blanket flower. See **Gaillardia.**

Bleeding heart. See **Dicentra.**

Blue marguerite. See **Felicia.**

Brachycome iberidifolia

Swan River daisy
Annual
Pictured on page 35

Cheerful and airy, Swan River daisy provides masses of color for edgings, raised beds, and containers in late spring and early summer. Lacy-leafed plants bear large numbers of inch-wide blooms in soft shades of blue, white, rose, and bicolors.

Sow seeds in the garden or in large containers in spring when the danger of frost is past. Give them sun, good soil, and regular watering.

Brassica oleracea

Flowering cabbage
Annual
Pictured on page 27

Flowering cabbage combines beauty with palatability. Bred for the interesting colors and patterns of its foliage, it remains one of the few garden annuals that is also edible— you can eat it cooked or raw like ordinary cabbage. Each head grows about 10 inches wide and is basically blue green with marbling and edging in white, cream, rose, and purple in autumn and winter.

Sow seeds in starter pots about 6 weeks before you want to transplant into the garden. Time the transplanting for midsummer in cold-winter areas and for late summer in mild-winter areas. Set plants in the garden about 15–18 inches apart in full sun. Keep soil moist.

Browallia

Amethyst flower
Annual
Pictured on page 29

This summer-long bloomer comes in two species offering blue, white, or violet flowers. The blue ones have white throats. *B. americana,* a branching plant, 1–2 feet high, has lopsided clusters of ½-inch blooms, resembling lobelias. *B. speciosa* is sprawling in growth, 2–3 feet high, with larger, petunialike blooms 1½–2 inches across. Bushy dwarf varieties of *B. speciosa* grow 12–15 inches high.

Sow seeds in flats indoors, 8–10 weeks prior to warm weather. At 70°–75°F / 21°–24°C, they should sprout in about 2 weeks. Don't transplant outdoors until all shade trees are in full leaf; then set young plants where they'll get afternoon shade.

Apply plenty of fertilizer. Give ample water, particularly during hot weather. Versatile browallia will continue to bloom through winter if brought indoors as a houseplant.

Browallia

Bush morning glory. See **Convolvulus.**

Busy Lizzie. See **Impatiens.**

Butterfly flower. See **Schizanthus.**

Butterfly weed. See **Asclepias.**

C

Calceolaria

Pocketbook flower
Perennial; usually grown as annual
Pictured on pages 21, 29

Clusters of bright little pouchlike flowers give shade-loving calceolaria its common name of pocketbook flower. Its blooms are yellow or red, often spotted with red or orange brown, in spring and summer. Although plants are perennial in areas with little frost, they are often set out as bedding plants in spring and discarded at the end of summer.

Where they are available, set out plants in the garden in a shady spot or in containers. Give them good soil and average water.

Calendula

Pot marigold
Annual
Pictured on pages 17, 37, 44

Nicknamed "pot marigold" because its leaves were once cooked as a vegetable and it resembles the more familiar marigold, cool-season calendula provides sunny color in spring, autumn, and mild-winter gardens.

The bushy plant has long, slender leaves, aromatic and slightly sticky. Growing 1–3 feet tall, it puts forth single, double, or semi-double blooms, one to a stem. The big-rayed flowers, 2½–4½ inches across, run a color gamut from cream, yellow to apricot, gold, and persimmon.

Where winters are cold, start seeds indoors (they take about a week to germinate), then transplant carefully in spring; or sow outdoors in early summer for color in late summer through autumn. In milder regions, sow outdoors in July or August for bloom by Christmas, or in September or October for spring bloom. Nurseries also offer plants in season.

Sun-loving calendulas tolerate poor soil, but need good drainage. Water regularly, without soaking. Protect from slugs and snails.

California poppy. See **Eschscholzia.**

Calla. See **Zantedeschia.**

Calliopsis. See **Coreopsis.**

Callistephus chinensis

China aster
Annual
Pictured on page 44

Summer gardens for cutting flowers are not complete without asters. Their big frilly flowers in shades of red, pink, white, lavender blue, and purple are sturdy and long lasting in vases and arrangements. Plants grow 1–3 feet high; blooms are 2–7 inches wide, depending on the variety. Use the low-growing kinds as edging plants, taller ones for cutting.

Sow seeds in the garden after danger of frost is past. Choose a spot with rich, well-drained soil in full sun. Give regular watering, but avoid overwatering plants where drainage is slow. Control leafhoppers to prevent the spread of aster yellows, a virus disease.

Campanula

Bellflower
Biennial. Perennial, hardy to −30°F/−34°C
Pictured on page 57

Among the campanulas are many fine and popular garden plants ranging from 6-inch ground covers to 6-foot flowering sentinels. Flowers can be bell-shaped, cupped, wide open, even star shaped; prevailing colors are blue, lavender, purple, and white. Most plants are clump forming with upright stems. They tend to be rosettes or tufts of leaves from which flowering stems arise bearing smaller stem leaves.

The best-known biennial is *C. medium* or Canterbury bells. Plants in bloom are upright 2–4 feet high, with long, loose clusters of 2–3-inch bells in typical colors plus pink; foliage is narrow and pointed. There is a double strain, 'Calycanthema', and there are annual kinds.

Two short-lived perennials that may be regarded as biennials are *C. barbata* and *C. pyramidalis*. The former is an upright plant (up to 1½ feet high) for foreground planting; it produces many stems topped by a few nodding, 1-inch lavender bells. Chimney bellflower, *C. pyramidalis*, is strictly for the background or accent: a stem rises to 6 feet from a clump of heart-shaped leaves. Each stem bears wide open star-pointed cups in blue or white.

Perennial bellflowers are generally two types: low-spreading and upright. Most aggressive spreader is Serbian bellflower *(C. poscharskyana)*. Clumps of heart-shaped leaves (like those of violets) spread by rooting runners; starlike lavender blue flowers appear along semi-upright stems. Similar, but lower and tidier, with smaller gray to green leaves is *C. elatines garganica*. Dalmatian bellflower *(C. portenschlagiana)* also is low and spreading with several inch-long, broadly bell-shaped, blue violet flowers per stem. *C. carpatica* forms low clumps of rather narrow foliage from which rise fairly upright stems 8–12 inches high, with cuplike bells in white or blue shades. Also upright, but to 1½ feet, *C. rotundilfolia* has branching stems of 1-inch nodding bells in white, blue, or purple. *C. glomerata*, with its clumps of wide, pointed leaves, is noted for tight clusters of flaring bells on 1–2-foot stems.

Peach-leafed bluebell (*C. persicifolia*) has a slender grace about its narrow leaves and slim 2–3-foot stems. Branched stems carry many outward-facing cupped bells in blue, white, or pink. *C. lactiflora* may send flowering stems to 5 feet high with rounded or domed clusters of broad, starry bells at stem tips. Leaves are lance shaped, about 3 inches long.

Campanulas need regular watering, good but well-drained soil, and light shade or filtered sunlight. In cool-summer and coastal gardens though, full sun is possible. Dig and divide clumps when they become crowded and less productive — in early spring where winters are cold, autumn or early spring in mild-winter regions.

Candytuft. See **Iberis.**

Canna

Perennial, hardy to 20°F/−7°C

Cannas contribute tropical splendor to the summer garden. In early spring, rhizomes send up thick stems bearing broadly oval, sheathing leaves 1–2 feet long. These stems end in spikes of irregularly shaped, flashy flowers: cream, yellow, orange, red, apricot, pink, and red and yellow combinations. Some varieties and strains are dwarf to 2–3 feet, while the more familiar old hybrids reach about 6 feet. Plants are evergreen in frost-free areas; elsewhere, sharp frost kills leaves and stems back to the ground.

Give cannas good well-drained soil, plenty of water, and full sun. Where rhizomes won't survive winter outdoors, dig clumps in autumn, dry rhizomes for a few days, then store them in sawdust in a cool (but not freezing) place until the following

Canna

year. After date of last expected hard frost, plant rhizomes 4 inches deep.

Canterbury bell. See **Campanula.**

Cape forget-me-not. See **Anchusa.**

Cape marigold. See **Dimorphotheca.**

Cardinal climber. See **Ipomoea.**

Cardinal flower. See **Lobelia.**

Carnation. See **Dianthus.**

Catharanthus roseus (Vinca rosea)

Madagascar periwinkle
Perennial, usually treated as an annual

For a sturdy dependable plant to grow in a hot, dry location, it's hard to beat periwinkle. It thrives on heat, sending up 5-petaled, 1½-inch-wide flowers from summer until frost. Leaves are glossy, dark green, 1–3 inches long; plants are bushy, 1–2 feet tall. Flower colors include white, white with red or pink eye, and pink.

Sow seeds in the garden, or set out plants in spring when danger of frost is past. Plants need average soil and little water once established. They'll grow in full sun or light shade.

Catmint. See **Nepeta.**

Celosia argentea

Cockscomb
Annual
Pictured on page 30

Planted judiciously, celosia can paint your garden with brushstrokes of breathtaking brilliance. Planted haphazardly, it may create a riot of strident, clashing colors.

Two kinds of hybrids are available: plume celosia and true cockscomb. The former makes the best background plant, though dwarf forms also make spectacular edgings. Growing as high as 3 feet, plume celosia shoots up feathery flower clusters ranging from scarlet to orange to deep gold.

True or crested cockscomb has velvety flowers arranged in fan-shaped clusters, in shades of pink, vivid red, and gold. Newer types grow 1½–2 feet tall, dwarf forms only 6–8 inches.

Bedding plants grow rapidly in full sun, the hotter the better; celosia won't tolerate shade. Seeds should not be planted outdoors until the soil is warm.

Centaurea

Annual. Perennial, hardiness varies (see individual descriptions)
Pictured on pages 17, 21, 29, 32

Annual centaureas are the familiar cornflower or bachelor's button and sweet sultan. Cornflower (*C. cyanus*) typically grows 2–3 feet high and bears bright blue flower heads about 1½ inches wide above narrow gray green leaves. Modern strains include flowers in pink shades, wine red, white; bicolored flowers; and shorter plants to about 1 foot high. Sweet sultan (*C. moschata*) has thistlelike flower heads in lavender to pink, plus white and yellow; they're 2-inches wide on upright, branching, 2–3-foot plants with deeply toothed green leaves.

Seeds of annual centaureas can be sown in place in the garden: cornflower in early autumn where winters are mild, early spring where ground freezes in winter; and sweet sultan in spring. They prefer a fairly light, non-acid soil, full sun, and moderate watering.

Among the perennial centaureas, some are grown for flowers, others for decorative foliage. Those grown for flowers are hardy to about −30°F/ −34°C. Persian cornflower, *C. dealbata*, is a robust 2-footer with deeply cut green leaves and fringy 2-inch flower heads in bright purplish pink during summer. Mountain bluet, *C. montana*, is shorter and more spreading, with more open flower heads in blue, pink, white, or purplish shades in late spring; leaves are narrow and green. Something of a curiosity is *C. macrocephala*, a coarse-textured, summer-flowering, 4-foot plant bearing large, fluffy, bright yellow flower heads that can be cut and dried. Garden requirements are the same as for annual centaureas.

The decorative foliage types are hardy to about −10°F/−23°C. *C. cineraria* (*C. candidissima*) is one of several plants called Dusty miller. It forms compact clumps 1–1½ feet high of strap-shaped, lobed, velvety white leaves. Summer flowers are usually purple, occasionally yellow. Trim back after flowering to keep plants compact. Take cuttings in spring or summer to start new plants. Velvet

centaurea, *C. gymnocarpa*, also is called Dusty miller. Taller, to 3 feet, it has the same velvety white leaves, but deeply cut rather than lobed. Flower heads are purple. Trim back and take cuttings as for *C. cineraria*. Both of these Dusty millers prefer a neutral, well-drained soil and moderate watering.

Centranthus ruber

Red valerian, Jupiter's beard
Perennial, hardy to −25°F/−32°C
Pictured on page 50

Most often seen as a pretty roadside weed, centranthus is surprisingly beautiful and rewarding in a garden. Bushy clumps of stems to 3 feet high have pointed, 4-inch, grayish blue green leaves. At the end of each stem is a fluffy, elongated cluster of tiny flowers: white, dusty pink, or crimson. Colors are bright yet soft.

Centranthus survives in poor soils with little water but grows more vigorously with decent soil and moderate watering. Plants seed themselves prolifically, so trim off old bloom clusters (this will also prolong the bloom season). Old clumps may be dug and separated in spring, but the easiest way to get new plants is to dig up volunteer seedlings.

Cerastium tomentosum

Snow-in-summer
Perennial, hardy to −35°F/−37°C
Pictured on page 59

This low-growing plant can be used as a ground cover or to edge a flower border, fill in between other perennials or shrubs, or grow between paving stones. Plants form spreading mats of ¾-inch silver gray, oval leaves that grow up to 8 inches high. One plant may spread 3 feet in a year. Masses of small white flowers in early summer provide the "snow."

Remarkably adaptable, cerastium thrives from seacoast to desert, in mild to frigid-winter regions. Give it light shade in hot summer areas, otherwise full sun. Good drainage is the main soil requirement. Regular watering causes fast growth, but established plantings get along with very little. Plantings may get shabby after several years; dig up and replant strong-rooted pieces — in early

spring where winters are coldest, autumn to spring elsewhere.

Cheddar pink. See **Dianthus.**

China aster. See **Callistephus.**

Chinese pink. See **Dianthus.**

Christmas rose. See **Helleborus.**

Chrysanthemum

Annual. Perennial, hardy to −30°F/−34°C
Pictured on pages 21, 27, 28, 29, 31, 34, 45

Under this heading are an annual — summer chrysanthemum — and several familiar perennials: painted daisy, Shasta daisy, feverfew, marguerite, and, of course, the autumn-blooming florists' chrysanthemum. All are basically daisies.

Summer chrysanthemums (*C. carinatum*) bloom in summer and autumn: 2-inch-wide flowers of purple, orange, pink, red, yellow, and white with contrasting rings around a dark center. Plants are 1–3 feet tall. Sow seeds in spring in full sun, almost any soil. Give regular watering.

All the perennials appreciate full sun, good well-drained soil, and plenty of water during the growing season. Most, unless noted below, need to be renewed every year or two. Divide and separate clumps in early spring, keeping only the strongest plants. You can start new plants from spring cuttings of florists' chrysanthemum, marguerite, and feverfew.

Painted daisy or pyrethrum (*C. coccineum*), flowering in mid- spring, has single or double blooms in white, pink, and red. They come on slender stems from dense, bushy plants with finely cut green foliage. Overall height is 2–3 feet. Divide plants in summer, after flowering.

Marguerite (*C. frutescens*) is a shrubby perennial, hardy only to about 20°F/−7°C. Rapid growth results in mounding plants up to 4 feet high and wide, covered with coarsely cut green leaves and dotted with daisies: single or double, white, cream, yellow, or pink. They're good in containers or wherever you want the effect of a profusely flowering shrub during spring and summer. Where they can live over winter, cut plants back lightly and often to prevent legginess and promote continued flowering. Cut back old plants more heavily in early spring, but not to leafless wood.

Shasta daisy (*C. maximum*) forms robust clumps of linear, tooth-edged leaves that push up leafy flower stalks in late spring and early summer. Original sorts were single white with big gold centers — 3–4-inch flowers on 3-foot stems. Named selections include semidouble and double-flowered types, some with fringed or quilled petals, a few with creamy white flowers, and dwarfs to about 15 inches high. Plants prefer filtered sunlight where summers are hot and dry. Divide clumps every 2–3 years in early spring.

Florists' chrysanthemum (*C. morifolium*) is the mainstay of the autumn garden. The result of centuries of plant breeding, they come in dazzling colors (except blue), flower forms, and flower and plant sizes. Low-growing cushion types will form compact plants covered with bloom. But the more extravagant, large-flowered sorts need frequent pinching during the growing season (until midsummer) to encourage bushiness and big blooms. Even then, they probably will need staking to remain upright during blooming. It's best to divide clumps early each spring or start new plants then from cuttings.

Feverfew (*C. parthenium*) forms fluffy clumps of lobed, rather feathery and aromatic leaves. In summer, leafy stems 2–3 feet long bear large clusters of small white or yellow daisies. Plant in full sun or light shade.

Cineraria. See **Senecio.**

Clarkia

Annual
Pictured on page 33

Clarkia includes those western wildflowers formerly known as godetia. It puts on a showy display from late spring into summer in cool-summer climates, but does less well in humid areas where summer temperatures rise above 80°F/27°C.

In the wild, clarkia usually has single cup-shaped flowers, but breeders have developed splendid double flowers in mixtures that include white, lavender, pinks and reds, and yellow. The spiky reddish stalks grow in mounds, 1–4 feet tall, and have small, narrow leaves.

C. amoena (Godetia) grows as

1–2½-foot-high mounds. Buds open into single or double flowers, usually bicolored with red or white streaks on pink, rose, or salmon.

Like other wildflowers, these require little care in a suitable location and climate. Sow seeds in the garden in early spring, or during the autumn in mild winter areas. Scatter seeds so plants will grow in clumps.

Cleome spinosa

Spider flower
Annual

Large and shrublike, cleome makes an attractive hedge and is one of the few annuals that grows easily in all 50 states. Many flowers cluster together along the top 1–2 feet of stem. They bloom through summer into autumn. The flowers burst forth in shades of pink, rose, and white, fluttering extremely long stamens and long thin seed pods that form beneath the blooms.

Cleome needs plenty of room. In warm areas, plants grow as tall as 6 feet, spreading 4–5 feet wide. Use cleome for backgrounds or in large patio tubs; it goes well against solid walls.

Only where summers are very short do you need to start seeds indoors. Otherwise, they'll sprout readily in warm soil outdoors, and the resulting plants will grow rapidly in full sun. Keep cleome on the dry side, or it becomes rank.

Cockscomb. See **Celosia.**

Coleus

Annual
Pictured on page 21

Prized for its vivid and brilliant leaves, coleus is a perennial usually grown as a bedding annual in cold-winter climates. It's also a very popular house plant.

The coarsely toothed, oval leaves come in both single and variegated colors — brown, chartreuse, green, red, magenta, maroon, orange, yellow, and purple. Plant outdoors in spring in lightly shaded borders or in containers, and bring cuttings indoors to grow in pots during winter.

Plant coleus from seeds or cuttings. With seeds, you get best results by planting indoors in flats. For best

colors, transplant to warm, rich, well-drained soil that receives strong, indirect light or moderate shade. Water generously, and feed regularly with high nitrogen fertilizer.

Columbine. See **Aquilegia.**

Coneflower. See **Rudbeckia.**

Confederate violet. See **Viola.**

Convallaria majalis

Lily-of-the-valley
Perennial, hardy to −30°F/−34°C; needs winter temperatures below 32°F/0°C

Plant consists of two pointed leaves, each 6–8 inches long and up to 3 inches wide. Each plant produces a flowering stem 6–8 inches long and lined with fragrant, plump white bells with scalloped edges. Under favorable conditions, it will spread to form a ground-covering colony.

Lily-of-the-valley prefers good soil enriched with organic matter and an annual top-dressing of compost or manure. These good woodland plants do best in filtered sunlight, but will take full sun where summers are not hot and dry. Regular watering gives best results but plants will survive with only moderate amounts of water. Individual plants (called *pips*) have a single growth point and somewhat fleshy roots. Sometimes pips are sold in clumps. Plant pips about 1½ inches deep, 5 inches apart. Early autumn planting is best in coldest regions; late autumn is best where ground doesn't freeze.

Convallaria

Convolvulus

Morning glory. See Ipomoea for vining morning glory
Annual. Perennial, hardy to 5°F/ −15°C
Pictured on page 59

Summer-blooming annual *C. tricolor* (bush morning glory) forms a lax, bushy plant to 1 foot high and 2 feet wide. Leaves are small, narrow ovals; blossoms are nearly flattened trumpets about 1½ inches across. Usual color is blue shading to white with a yellow throat; red 'Crimson Monarch' and bright blue 'Royal Ensign' are commonly available varieties. Plant seeds after soil has lost winter chill; nick tough seed coat with a knife for quicker germination. Give plants full sun, well-drained soil, and only moderate watering.

Ground morning glory, *C. mauritanicus,* is a border or groundcover perennial growing about 1½ feet high and spreading to 3 feet. Lavender blue, 1-inch blossoms come over a long period: late spring into autumn. Softly hairy gray green leaves are a pleasing backdrop for blossoms. Grow in full sun, preferably in well-drained soil with moderate watering, or in clay soils with infrequent watering.

Coral bells. See **Heuchera.**

Coreopsis

Annual. Perennial, most hardy to −30°F/−34°C
Pictured on pages 35, 50

Sunny yellow daisies decorate easy-to-grow plants in late spring, through summer, and even into autumn. Leaf texture varies from finely cut to narrow and linear; flowers are airily poised atop wiry stems. They bloom profusely and tend to set seed prolifically, so be sure to remove old flowers.

C. tinctoria (Calliopsis) is an annual. It's available in various strains that range from foot-high dwarfs to tall 3-footers, and in colors of solid yellow, orange, bronze through maroon shades, and yellow with contrasting dark inner band. All blooms have dark centers. Sow seeds in the garden in early spring in a sunny location. Plants prefer dryish soil.

Among the perennials, *C. au-*

riculata 'Nana' forms widely spreading clumps about 6 inches high, carrying 2-inch yellow orange flowers above the foliage. Taller, 1–3 feet, and spreading to 3 feet across, is *C. grandiflora* and its varieties. Flowers are bright yellow, up to 3 inches across, nearly double in 'Sunray' and semidouble in 'Sunburst.' Dwarf variety 'Goldfink' forms tufted clumps about 8 inches high with flowers just above the foliage. *C. lanceolata* is a low-growing plant, but stems rise to 2 feet with blossoms 1–2 inches across. *C. verticillata* forms mounding plants, 1–2 feet tall, consisting of finely divided foliage and 2-inch flowers.

All kinds of coreopsis are trouble-free, thriving even in fairly poor (but well-drained) soil and, when established, on little water. If clumps become crowded, divide them in early spring.

Cornflower. See **Centaurea.**

Corsican hellebore. See **Helleborus.**

Cosmos

Annual
Pictured on pages 19, 35, 45

Daisylike cosmos blossoms are borne on pliant stems, 2–6 feet high. Their height makes them excellent background plants; they also group attractively among equally lofty shrubs. Deceptively fragile-looking, they bob rather than break under gusts of wind, adding dance motions to your garden scenery.

The common cosmos (*C. bipinnatus*) has single flowers, 2–3 inches across, in shades of magenta, pink, white, and lavender, with tufted yellow centers. Another species, *C. sulphureus,* puts forth semidouble and double flowers in gold and vermilion, some with striped petals. Sow seeds from early spring through midsummer in full sun, in soil that is only moderately rich. For earliest bloom, sow in flats during late winter and transplant later. Seeds come in single colors, or mixed.

Cut freshly opened cosmos blossoms for bouquets; plunge them immediately into cool water to keep flowers and lacy foliage from wilting.

Cottage pink. See **Dianthus.**

Cranesbill. See **Geranium.**

Cup flower. See **Nierembergia.**

Cypress vine. See **Ipomoea.**

D

Dahlia merckii

Bedding dahlia
Perennial; treated as annual
Pictured on page 60

Start bedding dahlias from seed and you'll have flowers the same year, as well as more seeds and tubers that you can use to propagate new plants the next year. These compact plants grow 15–24 inches high. They have double, semi-double, or single 2–3-inch flowers in abundance all summer. Clear, luminous colors range from yellows and oranges to rich reds and purples.

In cold regions, start seeds indoors. They sprout rapidly after the weather warms and require only 6 to 8 weeks to grow big enough to plant outside. Seedlings transplant very well. In warmer areas, sow seeds directly in open ground. Bedding dahlias are also available at nurseries.

Dahlias appreciate rich, well-drained soil and full sun. In very hot areas they'll also need light afternoon shade. Water frequently.

Daylily. See **Hemerocallis.**

Delphinium

Perennial, hardy to −30°F/−34°C
Pictured on pages 38, 63

Delphiniums need special care for best results, even where the climate is well suited to them, but the rewards are worth the effort. Towering spires of rounded blossoms encompass some of the most penetrating shades of blue to be found in the summer garden.

Most nurseries and catalogs offer hybrid strains and individual named hybrids rather than species. Colors include light to dark blue, lavender, violet, purple, raspberry, pink, and white. Some kinds have small petals of contrasting color (called "bees") in the center of each flower. Plants range in height from 2–8 feet. The most widely available kinds include Blackmore and Langdon strain, Pacific Coast hybrids, Wrexham hybrids, Bishop hybrids, and Connecticut Yankee.

Delphiniums do best in an "English climate" with cool to warm (not hot) humid summers as in the Pacific coast fog belt, the Pacific Northwest (west of the Cascades), and—where winters permit—northern New England. Success diminishes where summers are hotter and drier.

They want a rich, well-drained soil, neutral to slightly alkaline. Roots should never dry out, but too much moisture invites crown rot. Full sun is best, although in hot areas, dappled sunlight would be better. Slugs and snails consider plants a delicacy, so keep bait handy.

Plant tall delphiniums in a sheltered location (to prevent blowing over) and stake them when flower spikes start to lengthen. When a spike has finished, cut it off just below the lowest flower; new growth then will begin at the plant's base. When new shoots are about 6 inches tall, cut out the old flowering spike entirely and apply a complete fertilizer around the plant. The new shoots will give a second bloom in late summer or early autumn.

Even with the best care, modern delphinium hybrids tend to be short-lived perennials. Clumps may be divided and separate plants set out in rejuvenated soil, but many gardeners prefer to start anew with young seedlings or cutting-grown plants. Delphiniums can be treated as annuals by planting them in autumn (in mild-winter regions) or early spring (anywhere) to flower in summer. This is the best way to grow delphiniums in areas with hot summers and/or mild winters.

Dianthus

Carnation, Pink, Sweet William
Annual. Biennial. Perennial, hardiness varies
Pictured on pages 28, 29, 31

These flowers have been favorites for several centuries. Not only do they have cheerful colors, and striking patterns, but nearly all of them also have a strong, spicy, clovelike scent. Flowers may be single, semi-double, or fully double; blooms are circular in outline, often with fringed petals. Summer is the main bloom time.

Sweet William (*D. barbatus*), is a biennial (planted in summer for flow-ers the following year), though annual strains are available. Single blossoms come in dense clusters ranging from 4–20 inches high. Flowers are about ½ inch across, in white, pink shades, red, purple, and striking bicolors (usually concentric bands of color). Leaves are green and narrowly lance shaped, unlike the more grasslike and grayish or bluish green leaves of other dianthus.

Carnations (*D. caryophyllus*), hardy to about -10°F/-23°C, are the largest members of the group and are perennial. Long-stemmed, highly fragrant florist carnations need good care to reach florist perfection in a garden. They have narrow grayish leaves up to 4 inches long and tend to be leggy and sprawly. They need stakes or a discreet fencelike enclosure to keep them upright and compact. To get larger blooms, disbud plants to leave only the terminal flower bud on each stem. Colors are white, cream, yellow, orange, red, pink, purple, and variegated combinations. Border carnations are similar to florist carnations, but they're bushier, more compact plants with slightly smaller flowers.

Pinks are shorter (about 6–18 inches high) and have smaller flowers and foliage than carnations. Most are perennial, hardy to about -30°F/-34°C. Short-lived *D. chinensis* usually is treated as an annual although it may live for 2–3 years. Perennial pinks include *D. allwoodii, D. deltoides* (Maiden pink), *D. gratianopolitanus* (Cheddar pink), *D. plumarius* (Cottage pink). Colors include white, pink shades (from lilac to salmon), red shades, purple, and many beautiful combinations. All but *D. chinensis* are famously fragrant.

All dianthus prefer cool to moderate summer temperatures. Full sun is best except where summers are hot. There they need light afternoon shade. Soil should not be acid; it should be well enriched, light and well drained. Plants need moderate watering. Remove spent flowers as they fade, breaking off stems at nodes where new growth is starting. Perennial kinds are easy to start from tip cuttings of new growth placed in a sandy rooting medium or directly in light garden soil. Carnations, particularly the florist types, become woody and decline in vigor after several years; by making stem cuttings you can keep new vigorous plants coming along. The pinks can be divided, but cuttings are the easiest way to get new plants. Best winter protection for foliage in cold climates is a layer of evergreen boughs.

Dicentra

Bleeding heart
Perennial, hardy to −30°F/−34°C; not for mild-winter/hot-summer areas
Pictured on page 49

Heart-shaped flowers with projecting tips hang from stems like jewels from a necklace. Combined with finely cut, almost feathery foliage, the whole effect is of grace and delicacy. Several species, named selections, and hybrids are available.

D. eximia forms fluffy clumps of blue gray foliage to 18 inches high, bearing deep pink flowers from midspring into summer. There is a white form, and the hybrid 'Bountiful' has nearly red flowers and darker foliage. Another hybrid, 'Luxuriant,' has dark blue green foliage to about 10 inches high with stalks of large, deepest pink blossoms carried well above the leaves. *D. formosa* spreads widely with suitable conditions. Its blue green foliage is about a foot high; the pale to deep rose flowers on stalks rise several inches above it. *D. spectabilis* is the best known and largest bleeding heart—2–3 feet high when in flower. Leaves are soft green and rise up the flowering stems; blooms are rose pink with white protruding tips. Variety 'Pantaloons' has pure white flowers.

Dicentras prefer a light, well-drained soil enriched with organic matter; roots need cool and moist (but not soggy) soil. Most species and hybrids prefer filtered sunlight to part shade, especially where summers are hot, but in cooler regions *D. spectabilis* and the hybrid 'Luxuriant' will succeed in full sun. Except in mild-winter areas where it does poorly, *D. spectabilis* can grow undisturbed for many years. Other kinds may need dividing after several years. Do this in earliest spring; take care not to break brittle roots.

Dietes

Fortnight lily
Perennial, hardy to 20°F/−7°C

Formerly known as moraea, these are the southern-hemisphere equivalent of the iris. Individual plants are fans of narrow, irislike leaves, and a clump looks like evergreen Siberian irises. Wiry, branching flower stalks produce a succession of blooms through spring and summer; each flower lasts for one day. Individual blossoms are flat and 6-petaled.

D. bicolor has light yellow 2-inch flowers with pea-size maroon spots on outer petals; it grows to about 3 feet high. D. vegeta (D. iridioides) has 3-inch blooms of white with brown purple spots surrounded by an orange ring. It grows up to 4 feet, with flower stalks that bloom for several years.

All dietes grow well in full sun to light shade and in average soil. Best performance comes with regular watering, but established plants will endure drought and poor soil (particularly D. vegeta).

Digitalis

Foxglove
Biennial or perennial, hardy to −20°F/−29°C
Pictured on pages 35, 63

Stately spires of foxgloves, their thimble-shaped flowers suspended from the top 2 feet of spikes 5–8 feet high, were conspicuous components of old-fashioned cottage gardens. They were biennials that grew in one year and flowered in the next. Now plant breeders have greatly broadened our choices: "dwarfs" that reach only 3 feet, flowers that flare more widely and stand at nearly right angles to the spike, strains that bloom in one year, a wider range of colors, and perennial species.

Common foxglove, D. purpurea, is the basic biennial species. Plants are clumps of large, furry, tongue-shaped leaves from which tall, flowering spikes emerge in spring to early summer. Colors include purple, lilac pink, white, strong pink, yellow, and various pastels. Shortest strain is Foxy, which blooms as an annual only 5 months after it's been sown. Five-foot Excelsior strain has outward-facing flowers; Shirley strain has traditional height and aspect but a full range of colors; 4-foot Gloxiniiflora has larger, more wide-open flowers. Another biennial is D. ferruginea with 6-foot spikes of inch-long yellowish blooms marked with rusty red netting.

Perennial foxgloves include D. grandiflora (D. ambigua) which has

brown-marked, pale yellow, 3-inch flowers on spikes 2–3 feet tall; and D. mertonensis in deep rose color, also 2–3 feet tall.

Both biennial and perennial types need filtered sun to light shade, good soil, and regular watering. Set out perennials in early spring. Plant biennials in summer or autumn (as soon as plants are available) for bloom the following summer, or sow seeds in spring for plants that will flower the next year. Cut off flowering spikes after bloom to stop seed production and stimulate new flowering stems. Slugs and snails may attack leaves.

Dimorphotheca

African daisy, Cape marigold
Annual

A number of species and varieties grow 6–12 inches high, spreading in solid mounds. Glossy, daisylike flowers, 2½–4 inches across, come in mixed colors—apricot, rose, salmon, white, yellow, as well as white with a blue black center ringed with blue. Blossoms open only in full sun and close at night or in cloudy weather. In warm, dry climates, during winter and early spring, blossoms proliferate, sometimes obscuring foliage. More humid regions produce lush foliage but fewer blooms.

African daisies thrive on lots of sunshine, and on heat reflected from a nearby wall or fence. They require only light watering, and need no special care. In mild-winter climates, broadcast seeds in late summer so plants will produce buds before cold weather. In cold-winter areas, plant in spring for late summer blooms.

Dusty miller. See **Artemisia, Centaurea, Senecio.**

E

Echinacea purpurea

Purple coneflower
Perennial, hardy to −35°F/−37°C

This is the purple counterpart of gloriosa daisies. Its single daisy flowers have dark centers raised into a hump or cone and may be 4 inches wide. Typically, petals are purplish and bend downward from the center, but various named selections have

other colors and flatter flowers. In addition to 'White Lustre' with its golden center, there are varieties in rose and crimson red. Bloom comes in midsummer, on stems up to 4 feet tall, from full clumps of oval, 4–8-inch, sandpaper-textured leaves.

These are productive, trouble-free plants, needing only full sun, average but well-drained soil, and moderate watering. After 3 years, divide in spring or autumn.

Echinops exaltatus

Globe thistle
Perennial, hardy to about −30°F/−34°C

Globe thistle has deeply cut leaves up to a foot long, green above, but gray beneath, and prickly. They form a solid, upright clump about 4 feet high that is topped in summer with round, spiny-looking blue flowers. Seed-grown plants vary in quality of blue color; the variety 'Taplow Blue' is a good steel blue. Some catalogues list the species as E. ritro or E. sphaerocephalus.

Globe thistle makes a good cut flower and is attractive when dried if it's cut soon after heads show color. Plant in spring or autumn, preferably in light, well-drained soil. Give moderate watering, and divide clumps about every four years.

Echinops

Epimedium

Bishop's hat
Perennial, hardy to −30°F/−34°C; not suited to mild-winter regions of South, Southwest, and Southern California

Elegant, neat, polished, and tough are appropriate words for epimediums. They are fine border or small-scale ground-cover plants for part shade. Where summers are cool or moisture is abundant, they do well in sun. All have heart-shaped leaflets on wiry leaf stalks, with overlapping leaves that form a dense clump or cover. New spring growth is bronzy pink, becoming green by summer, and turning red bronze in autumn. Small cup-and-saucer-shaped flowers (some with spurs) are carried on airy open spikes on wiry stems.

Largest of the common epimediums is *E. pinnatum* which may reach 15 inches high; flowers are yellow or yellow and red. Reaching about 1 foot high, *E. grandiflorum* has the largest flowers (to 2 inches wide) in red and violet or, in selected forms, white, pink, or purple. Also about 1 foot high is *E. rubrum* with red and white flowers or, in named varieties, pink or white.

Epimediums appreciate a somewhat acid soil with lots of organic matter. In part shade they associate naturally with shade-loving plants, but they'll grow in full sun, if summers are not hot and dry, as long as they receive plenty of moisture. Clumps don't need dividing. To increase quantity of plants, cut through clump with a sharp spade and transplant separated chunks (with some soil). Do this in autumn or early spring.

Erigeron

Fleabane
Perennial, hardy to −20°F/−29°C, except as noted

These cheerful daisies are kin to perennial asters. One difference is that flower heads contain threadlike rather than flattened petals. Most widely sold are summer flowering *E. speciosus* and its hybrids. Blue to lavender shades are typical of *E. speciosus* — yellow-centered single blossoms to about 1½ inches across. Bushy plants reach 2 feet high, with rather narrow, pointed leaves. Among the named hybrids, some have flowers in white or shades of pink, violet, lavender, and blue. Some have flowers ranging from single to nearly double, and some plants are short — 1–2 feet tall.

A spreading ground cover or rock-wall plant is *E. karvinskianus*, hardy to about 20°F/−7°C. Pinkish white, ¾-inch flower heads dot the narrow-foliaged plants mainly in summer.

Give fleabanes light, well-drained soil, full sun to lightest shade, and moderate watering. In early spring, set out *E. speciosus* and hybrids and divide older, crowded clumps.

Eschscholzia californica

California poppy
Perennial, grown as annual
Pictured on page 33

Few flowers ask less and give more than the California poppy, which isn't a true poppy at all. The state flower of California, it covers hills and fields with wildflower abandon, especially in spring.

A perennial that's more often grown as an annual, the 1–2-foot plants have lacy, blue green foliage, willowy stems, and satiny, cup-shaped blossoms. Wild California poppies are single flowers of glowing golden orange, but breeders have developed hybrids with double or semi-double blossoms in cream, deep red, scarlet, pink, orange, and yellow.

Vigorous and easy to grow, their only requirement is light, well-drained soil and a sunny location. In autumn, where winters are mild, or in spring, where winters are cold, simply toss handfuls of seeds onto cultivated soil, and let the rain soak it in. After blooming as long as late summer, plants reseed themselves readily and, unless you remove their pods, may spread farther than you wish.

Euphorbia

Annual. Perennial, hardiness varies

The euphorbias present amazingly different appearances. Often, what appear to be flower petals are really modified leaves, called bracts, surrounding the tiny true flowers. All plants have a milky sap that is irritating to eyes and sensitive skin.

Snow-on-the-mountain (*E. marginata*) is a branching, lightweight plant to 2 feet tall. Its oval light green leaves have white margins and stripes; on upper parts of plants some leaves may be entirely white. In spring, sow seeds in the garden; plants will reseed themselves.

Of the more commonly grown perennial euphorbias, *E. characias*, hardy to about 5°F/-15°C, forms a clump of many stems up to 4 feet tall, each ringed with linear grayish blue green leaves. In late winter to early spring, the top of each stem produces a dome-shaped cluster of many 1-inch chartreuse bracts that remain attractive for several months. During spring, new stems grow from the base; cut off dead flower stems.

E. c. wulfenii (sometimes sold as *E. veneta*) has broader clusters of yellower bracts. *E. rigida* (*E. biglandulosa*), hardy to about 5°F/-15°C, is similar. Its stems angle outward, then upward to around 2 feet; gray green leaves that ring the stems are only about 1½ inches long.

For front of the border, try cushion spurge (*E. epithymoides*, sometimes sold as *E. polychroma*). Hardy to about −20°F/−29°C, plants form dense, rounded clumps 1–1½ feet high and wide. In spring, flattened clusters of greenish yellow bracts appear that last into summer; foliage turns reddish in autumn.

Perennial euphorbias will endure poor soil and scant water. Set out plants in spring in full sun.

Euryops

Perennial, hardy to 20°F/−7°C

Like marguerites (*Chrysanthemum frutescens*), these are shrubby daisies, but with a tougher look.

Lowest is *E. acraeus*, a 2-foot mound of short and slender silver gray, almost succulent looking foliage. Bright yellow, inch-wide daisies appear in late spring. Tallest, to 5–6 feet, is *E. athanasiae*. Its 3-inch bright yellow flowers, appearing in winter, contrast with the finely divided, fuzzy white leaves. Most familiar is the 3-foot *E. pectinatus* that has yellow daisies and gray green, finely divided foliage. Main bloom is late winter and spring, but scattered flowers may appear throughout the year.

All three euryops species need excellent drainage; otherwise they're not particular about soil. Water needs aren't great after plants are established. Plant in full sun. All take seacoast winds.

Evening primrose. See **Oenothera**.

Fairy primrose. See **Primula.**

False dragonhead. See **Physostegia.**

False spirea. See **Astilbe.**

Felicia amelloides

Blue marguerite
Perennial, hardy to 20°F/−7°C; grown as annual in cold-winter climates
Pictured on pages 20, 37

Similar to a marguerite (*Chrysanthemum frutescens*), this plant is a fast-growing, shrubby daisy. Cheery yellow-centered blue daisies come profusely on dense, mounding plants to 2 feet high and 4 feet wide. Oval, inch-long leaves have a rough texture. Main bloom season is summer, but where plant can be grown as a perennial, flowers continue throughout the year. There are varieties in several sizes and shades of blue.

Full sun, average soil, and routine watering are basic requirements. Where plants are perennial, cut them back severely at summer's end. Remove old flowers to encourage more blooms. Start new plants from cuttings of new growth.

Feverfew. See **Chrysanthemum.**

Flanders field poppy. See **Papaver.**

Flax. See **Linum.**

Fleabane. See **Erigeron.**

Floss flower. See **Ageratum.**

Flowering cabbage. See **Brassica.**

Flowering tobacco. See **Nicotiana.**

Forget-me-not. See **Myosotis.**

Fortnight lily. See **Dietes.**

Four o'clock. See **Mirabilis.**

Foxglove. See **Digitalis.**

Funkia. See **Hosta.**

Gaillardia

Blanket flower
Annual. Perennial, hardy to −30°F/−34°C

The warmth of summer and autumn is captured in the yellow, red, and bronze tints of these showy daisies.

Gaillardia

During summer and into autumn, perennial *G. grandiflora* produces showy 3–4-inch flowers — yellow to orange with dark centers, or red to bronze or maroon with yellow petal tips. Lance-shaped soft green leaves are rough to the touch. Mature plants reach 2–3 feet high, though 'Goblin' is only 1 foot high (good for front of a border). There are named strains and individual varieties in particular colors or combinations.

The annual types, *G. pulchella* and hybrid strains, include colors from nearly white to dark red plus bicolor combinations. Flowers are smaller — about 2 inches across — and there are strains that have ball-shaped blossoms instead of typical daisy flowers. Dwarf strains may be only a foot high, while taller sorts reach 2 feet with blossoms carried on wiry stems.

A good, but light and well-drained soil is a must — especially for perennial sorts that may rot in soggy winter soils. Both annual and perennial types thrive on heat and need only moderate watering. Sow seeds of annual gaillardias after danger of frost. Set out perennials either in autumn or spring. Early spring is preferable for dividing crowded clumps (after about three years).

Gayfeather. See **Liatris.**

Gazania

Perennial, hardy to 20°F/−7°C; grown as annual in cold-winter climates
Pictured on page 58

Gazanias are among the most colorful and varied perennials with daisy flowers. There are two kinds: clump forming and trailing. Plant breeders have been busy with both.

Among the clump-forming kinds you may find named hybrids, named strains, or just "gazanias" in mixed colors or in separate colors. Colors include white, cream, yellow, orange, red, pink, bronze and copper, dark red to purplish — sometimes with dark centers circled by contrasting rings of color. Blooms are generally single, 3–4 inches wide, on stems that rise 6–8 inches above clumps of linear to lobed leaves.

The trailing kinds, developed from *G. rigens leucolaena*, are similar except that they send out long trailing stems and their foliage is often silver gray.

In mildest areas, gazanias may bloom throughout the year, but peak bloom is in late spring and into summer. They aren't fussy about soil and need only moderate watering. Divide and reset plants about every three years. In areas where gazanias would freeze during winter, take cuttings in autumn; keep them indoors over winter.

Geranium

Cranesbill.
See also Pelargonium
Perennial, hardy to −30°F/−34°C

True geraniums are more modest and charming than their brightly colored, flashy cousins, the so-called geraniums that are really pelargoniums (see page 87). Plant sizes and habits vary, but all have 5-petaled, round flowers in white, pink, blue, violet, and purple shades — about 1–1½ inches across.

Under 6 inches high, but spreading, is *G. dalmaticum*. Small leaves are rounded and deeply lobed; flowers are soft pink or white. *G. endressii* forms dense mounds about 1½ feet high of deeply cut and lobed leaves and pink flowers. Of similar size and habit is *G. himalayense*, but blooms are violet blue with darker veins. Largest in leaf (to 6 inches, deeply lobed) and tallest (to 3 feet) is *G. pratense*. Usual flowers are violet blue with reddish veins. Mounding to a foot or more and spreading to 2 feet, *G. sanguineum* is a good foreground plant or small-scale ground cover. Flower color varies from purple to magenta, pink, and white; the variety 'Prostratum' (often sold as 'Lancastriense') is an especially good pink form.

Flowering season is late spring through summer, with *G. endressii* extending well into autumn. Good red autumn foliage color comes on *G.*

dalmaticum, G. pratense, and *G. sanguineum.*

Geraniums are best in full sun, except where summers are hot and dry, but they can get along in light shade. Give them good, well-drained soil and regular watering. Increase plants by taking cuttings in summer.

Gerbera jamesonii

Transvaal daisy
Perennial, hardy to 15°F/−9°C

These are daisies raised to the state of elegance. From clumps of tongue-shaped, lobed 10-inch leaves rise slender stems about 1½ feet high, each bearing one flawless, slender-petaled, 4-inch daisy. Colors span the warm range from cream to red, with numerous softly glowing corals, salmons, and terracottas. Basic flower has single ring of petals, but hybrid forms may have two such rows or may be completely double. Heaviest flowering is in early summer and in late autumn, but blooms may come at any time.

Gerberas need well-prepared and well-drained soil. Set out plants in full sun (or light shade in hot/dry summer areas) making sure to keep crowns of plants slightly above soil level to avoid crown rot. Plants appreciate frequent applications of fertilizer. Give deep watering, but allow soil to become nearly dry between waterings. Divide crowded clumps in late winter to early spring.

Geum

Perennial, hardy to −10°F/−23°C

Bright yellow, orange, and red are geum's colors. They're displayed in single to double, ruffly, rose-like blossoms carried in airy branched clusters that stand well above clumps of foliage. Individual plants are rosettes of hairy, divided leaves; established clumps form mounds of foliage slightly more than a foot high in some varieties.

Among the shorter geums is G. 'Borisii', with foot-high flower stalks of orange single flowers above clumps of rounded leaves. The hybrid 'Georgenberg' is similar in soft yellowish apricot. Selections of *G. quellyon* (sold also as *G. chiloense* and *G. coccineum*) lift their flowers to about 2 feet high and have long

leaves with many leaflets. Flowering time for all is midspring, but removing spent blossoms can encourage repeated bursts through summer.

Average well-drained soil, regular water, and full sun (light shade in hot/dry summer regions) will satisfy geums. If clumps become crowded or start to lose vitality, dig and divide in early spring.

Glechoma hederacea

Ground ivy
Perennial; usually treated as annual

Some people consider ground ivy to be a weed. Growing in the wrong place, it can be a nuisance, but combined in a container with other annuals, it is useful and interesting.

It's a trailing plant with pairs of kidney-shaped leaves along stems that can grow 18 inches or more. Ground ivy has small blue flowers in spring and summer, but its main value is as a foliage counterpoint to more flowery annuals.

Ground ivy is hard to find in nurseries. If possible, get a start from a friend. Where it's available, plant it in hanging containers with other annuals that like sun or light shade.

Globeflower. See **Trollius.**

Globe thistle. See **Echinops.**

Gloriosa daisy. See **Rudbeckia.**

Golden flax. See **Linum.**

Golden glow. See **Rudbeckia.**

Golden marguerite. See **Anthemis.**

Grape-leafed anemone. See **Anemone.**

Ground ivy. See **Glechoma.**

Gypsophila

Baby's breath
Annual. Perennial, hardy to −30°F/−34°C; not suited to the deep South or frost-free parts of Southwest
Pictured on pages 34, 35, 47

Airy is the word for baby's breath. Much-branched plants with small or sparse leaves bear a froth of small flowers that seem almost to float in space.

Annual baby's breath, *G. elegans,*

grows quickly to 1–2 feet high, with flowers of white or pink, depending on variety, but lasts only a short while in the garden. For flowers all summer, sow seeds in the garden every 3 to 4 weeks so that new plants will come along to replace the old.

More widely grown is perennial baby's breath, *G. paniculata.* Several varieties are available, varying from about 1½–4 feet high and with either white or pink double flowers from ¼ to ¾ inch across. All form billowy, mounded plants that bloom in summer. If spent blooms are removed, plants may continue to produce new flowers into early autumn. Baby's breath is a favorite cut flower, fresh or dried.

Plants need full sun in well-drained, nonacid soil, and should receive routine watering. Varieties of *G. paniculata* often are grafted plants; plant them so that graft union (swollen or gnarled part between roots and stems) is about an inch below soil level. Plants are tap-rooted: they never need digging or dividing.

H

Helenium autumnale

Sneezeweed
Perennial, hardy to −35°F/−37°C

Bright daisies in autumnal tints appear from midsummer to early autumn, a slump period in the garden after the rush of summer-flowering plants. Flowers usually consist of a single row of petals surrounding a dark, raised center. A number of named varieties are sold, ranging in height from 2 to about 4 feet, and in color from yellow through orange to copper and mahogany.

Heleniums need only average soil, but they do prefer it regularly moist, though not soggy. Full sun is best, and topnotch performance comes where summers are hot (as long as

Helenium

plants are watered). Since clumps become crowded quickly, dig and divide every 2–3 years in spring.

Helianthus

Sunflower
Annual. Perennial, hardy to −25°F/−32°C
Pictured on page 63

The best known sunflower is the gigantic, towering kind grown for its seeds. However, there are several ornamental selections of this annual that are smaller and more useful in gardens; and there are perennial sorts, too. All have round, flat flowers: a central disc surrounded by a ring of petals, or fully double with no disc showing. Leaves are rough textured with toothed edges.

Annual sunflowers (*H. annuus*) will perform respectably when grown in poor soil with little water, but they'll look their exuberant best in good soil with regular watering. The mammoth ones grown for seeds (usually sold as "Mammoth Russian") need the better care. Among the decorative varieties are double yellows ('Chrysanthemum-flowered', 'Sungold', 'Teddy Bear') as well as ones with orange and red brown blossoms. Sow seeds in garden in spring.

Perennial sunflowers may be sold as named selections of *H. decapetalus* or *H. multiflorus*. 'Flore Pleno' and 'Loddon Gold' are about 4 and 5 feet tall, respectively, with fully double bright blossoms about 4 inches across. Plants need full sun and same cultural requirements as annual types. Divide crowded clumps in early spring.

Helichrysum bracteatum

Strawflower
Annual
Pictured on page 47

Strawflowers come in glistening hues of orange, red, pink, white, and yellow. Their papery, pompomlike blossoms, 2½ inches across, top numerous long stems growing from each sturdy, 2–3-foot-tall plant. (Dwarf kinds are 12–18 inches tall; they have smaller flowers, and bloom sooner than tall kinds.)

The splashy blossoms make lovely fresh arrangements, but they are lovely as dry flowers, too. To dry them, cut the flowers before their yellow centers appear. Strip off the leaves, and bundle each color separately. Wrap bundles in a cone of newspaper; hang the cones upside down in a dry, shady place until dry.

Strawflowers are easy to grow. Plant seeds directly in the garden in late spring or early summer. They need full sun and fairly dry soil.

Hellebore. See **Helleborus**.

Helleborus

Hellebore
Perennial; hardiness varies

Hellebore offers a touch of class to lightly shaded or woodland gardens, and it blooms when few other plants are around to compete for attention. It has attractive foliage; flowers have 5 wide petals and big stamens.

Helleborus foetidus has the most graceful foliage: 7–9 blackish green leaflets per leaf. In late winter and early spring, plants bear clusters of 1-inch-wide green and purple flowers on 1½-foot-tall leafy stems. Plants are hardy to −10°F/−23°C.

Corsican hellebore, *H. lividus corsicus*, is tall, up to 3 feet high. Its leaves consist of 3 light blue green, broad-toothed leaflets. Large pale chartreuse flowers appear in late autumn in mild-winter regions, or early spring in cold-winter regions. This one will take less water and more sun than other hellebores. It's hardy to 5°F/−15°C.

Christmas rose (*H. niger*) will flower between December and early spring. Dark green, slightly toothed leaves contain 7–9 leaflets. Flowers, on leafless stems, are white, to 2 inches across, becoming purplish pink with age. It grows well in heavy, moist soil but must have winter chill to thrive; it's hardy to −30°F/−34°C. Lenten rose (*H. orientalis*), hardy to −30°F/−34°C, is similar but has larger, more toothed foliage, with 5–11 broad leaflets per leaf. Bloom starts in late winter and continues into spring. Flowers may be greenish or buff white, liver purple, or various pinkish shades, often with dark spots in the centers.

All hellebores appreciate rich soil. Give them woodland conditions: medium shade to filtered sunlight and regular watering. Plants do not like to be dug or divided, and will reestablish slowly if they're moved.

Hemerocallis

Daylily
Perennial, hardy to −35°F/−37°C
Pictured on page 36

Daylilies are among the most conspicuous and satisfying of the late-spring/early-summer perennials. Although each large, lilylike blossom lasts only one day, new flowers appear in seemingly tireless succession. Plants consist of arching strap-shaped leaves, which may explain their old-fashioned name, "corn lily."

The original daylilies were mostly yellow and orange, but modern hybrids come in many shades and colors. Average flower size is 4–6 inches on 2–3-foot stems. There are miniatures with flowers 3 inches or less across, on stems as short as 12 inches. There are also giants on 5-foot stems with proportionally large flowers. Many newer hybrids have broad petals that give a "full circle" appearance to their flowers. Many hybrids have flowers that remain open into the evening or until next morning, and some are rebloomers that give a second crop.

Modern daylilies grow easily and successfully in widely diverse climates. Plants may be totally deciduous, semievergreen, or totally evergreen. Deciduous ones may not be totally successful in frost-free regions; evergreen ones usually need winter protection in coldest areas.

Plant daylilies in full sun, filtered sunlight, or even part shade (especially where summers are hot and dry). Well-prepared soil and regular watering give best results, but daylilies will survive and perform even with some neglect. For best performance, divide when clumps become crowded—after 3–6 years—in fall or early spring where summers are hot, in summer where summers are cool or the growing season is short.

Heuchera

Coral bells, Alum root
Perennial, hardy to −30°F/−34°C; not suited to Florida and Gulf coast
Pictured on page 42

Coral bells have been favorites with generations of gardeners for their good-looking foliage and graceful, airy flower spikes. Nearly round leaves are scallop edged, forming low, mounded clumps. From these clumps emerge, in spring through summer, wiry, branched stalks 15 to 30 inches tall and bearing open clusters of small, bell-shaped flowers. Colors include shades of pink and red, white, and a variety aptly called 'Chartreuse'. All available coral bells are selections of *H. sanguinea* or hybrids of it with other species. They're best used in foreground plantings — as edging or even as small-scale ground cover.

Plants prefer sun, but need light shade where summers are hot and dry. Average garden soil and regular watering produce best results. Clumps become crowded in 3–4 years and plant crowns become elevated on short, thick stalks. Divide clumps in early spring in cold-winter regions, in autumn where winters are mild. When replanting rooted divisions, set crown of plant even with soil surface.

Hibiscus moscheutos

Rose-mallow
Perennial, hardy to −10°F/−23°C

Here is the splendor of the tropics in a fairly hardy perennial. Really big (6–12 inches across) morning-glory-type blossoms begin in early summer and may continue until frost. Plants are shrublike, upright from 3 to 6 feet or sometimes more, with large oval leaves. Colors are in the white, pink, red range, sometimes with a central eye of contrasting color. Individual named hybrids are sold, as are seed strains. They come as plants of mixed colors or as seeds which may bloom in the first year they're sown.

Average soil, full sun, and plenty of moisture are all that rose mallows need. Where summers are hot and

Hibiscus

dry, plants appreciate part shade and regular watering. Set crowns of new plants about 3 inches below soil surface. Clumps increase in size gradually but do not need periodic dividing.

Hollyhock. See **Alcea.**

Hosta

Plantain lily, Funkia
Perennial, hardy to −35°F/−37°C
Pictured on page 57

Although they produce flowers that are attractive in mass, hostas are valued more for their leaves. Foliage varies from grayish blue green to chartreuse. Sometimes leaves have white or cream margins or variegations, or white centers and green edges. Plants range from 4-inch miniatures to some that form clumps 5 feet across. Leaves arise directly from the ground and are heart shaped to pointed oval, on leaf stalks of different lengths so that plants form mounds of overlapping foliage. Summer flowers, in white, lavender, or blue, are trumpet to bell shaped. They're carried, outward facing or drooping, from the tops of slender stems.

Hostas will grow in sun or shade. Plants in sun produce more flowers, while those in shade may grow larger or taller. Where summers are hot and dry, part shade or shade is a necessity; but in regions where the air is humid during the growing season, hostas can thrive in sun. Best growth is in good soil, well prepared with organic matter. Water regularly, especially for plants in full sun. Control slugs and snails; they can ravage new foliage as it emerges in spring.

I

Iberis

Candytuft
Annual. Perennial, hardy to −30°F/−34°C

Both annual and perennial candytufts are time-tested favorites for trouble-free, colorful border plantings. All produce compact heads or short spikes of flowers that cover plants during bloom season.

Largest and tallest is annual *I. amara*, hyacinth-flowered candytuft.

Like hyacinths, the fragrant white blossoms come in compact spikes on plants reaching 1½ feet tall. Globe candytuft, *I. umbellata*, also annual, forms bushy, spreading plants — about 6 inches high in dwarf strains, twice as tall otherwise. Small flowers in compact, quarter-size clusters may be white, pink, or lavender. In mild-winter regions, sow seeds in garden in autumn or early spring, but only in early spring where winters are colder. Give plants full sun, average soil.

Perennial evergreen candytuft, *I. sempervirens,* will smother itself with 2-inch clusters of sparkling white flowers from early to late spring. Typically, plants are 8–12 inches high and twice as wide, but named strains include lower types and more wide-spreading ones. When not in bloom, plants are densely foliaged with glossy, narrow dark green leaves. Plant in full sun (or light shade in hottest areas) in good, well-drained soil, either in autumn or early spring. Give routine watering. After bloom, remove spent flowers to encourage new growth. Start new plants from stem cuttings in summer.

Iceland poppy. See **Papaver.**

Impatiens

Balsam, Busy Lizzie
Annual. Perennial grown as annual
Pictured on pages 21, 56

Thanks to efforts of plant breeders, this group of old-fashioned garden plants has a new look and usefulness. The colors are electric and the foliage of some kinds is just as colorful now as the flowers.

Balsam (*Impatiens balsamina*) is an old-favorite summer annual. Plants grow from 10–30 inches tall; leaves are 1½–6 inches long. Flowers appear on the stems among the leaves in colors of pink, red, lilac, and white. Some flowers resemble small double camellias.

Sow seeds in the garden after frost danger has passed in spring. Give plants rich, well-drained soil, full sunlight or light shade, lots of water.

Busy Lizzie (*Impatiens wallerana*), a tender perennial that's usually grown as an annual, gives bright color to shade gardens all summer. There are many kinds and sizes ranging from 4–8 inch dwarfs up to 2-foo' full-size varieties. Colors include red, pink, rose, violet, orange, white, and bicolors. Leaves are dark green and glossy on pale-green succulent stems.

In spring, you can set out nursery plants or start from seeds. Indoors, start seeds 6-8 weeks before the last frost date. Set out plants or sow seeds directly in the garden when the weather and soil are warm. Plant in shade in rich, moist soil.

New Guinea hybrids are the newest impatiens. Bred from species from New Guinea, they've brought increased color to flowers and especially to foliage. Flower colors include red, orange, pink, lavender, and purple; leaves are often striped with red or yellow. Together they make dazzling combinations. Plants grow 8–24 inches tall and are especially good in pots.

Set out plants when weather is reliably warm in spring. Give plants more sunlight than bedding impatiens, but not full, hot sun. Grow in good soil with ample water and fertilizer. Plants will bloom until frost kills them.

Ipomoea

Morning glory
Annual. Perennial, hardy to 20°F/−7°C

These morning glories are fast-growing vines. On sunny days their flowers open in the morning and close by afternoon. Each trumpet-shaped blossom flares out to a funnel or a flat, circular bell. Bloom season is summer.

Most familiar annual is *I. tricolor* with large, showy flowers in blue shades, lavender, pink, red, and white, usually with white or yellow throats. Some named varieties are sold. Leaves are heart shaped, and vines twine to about 10 feet. *I. nil* and varieties are similar. Moonflower (*I. alba*) produces 6-inch fragrant white flowers on a rampant 20–30-foot vine. Blossoms open after sundown and last until the following morning. Cypress vine or cardinal climber (*I. quamoclit*) has finely divided, threadlike foliage; its flowers are red slender tubes that flare into star-shaped funnels.

The perennial vine is blue dawn flower (*I. acuminata*). Flowers are 3–5 inches wide, in clusters, opening bright blue and fading to pink. Fast growing, it may reach 30 feet. Plants may be started from seeds, cuttings, layered branches, or division.

Morning glories are relatively undemanding. Give them average soil, full sun, moderate water. Plant seeds in the garden after last expected frost. Germination is faster if you notch the hard seed coats with a knife or file, or if you soak seeds in warm water for a few hours before planting.

Iris

Perennial, hardiness varies
Pictured on pages 22, 37, 53

Irises are the showoffs in any spring flower display. Their flowers consist of three upright petals called "standards" and three horizontal or drooping petal-like sepals called "falls." In Louisiana and Japanese irises, the standards may assume the same position as the falls, and in double Japanese irises you can hardly distinguish between the two. Iris flowers are of two types: bearded, in which a caterpillarlike "beard" extends onto the fall, and beardless.

Tall bearded irises are the most widely grown. They carry their showy flowers on branching stems 28–48 inches tall. Color range includes all but true green and scarlet red, and combinations of colors abound. Peak bloom ranges from mid-April, where winters are mild, to early June in coldest winter regions. Smaller kinds of bearded iris include miniature dwarfs, standard dwarfs, intermediates, and miniature tall bearded irises. Collectively, they range from 4–28 inches tall.

Bearded irises *must* have well-drained soil in the slightly acid to somewhat alkaline range. Prepare soil well with organic amendments and fertilizer. Set out plants in full sun, in summer where winters are cold, in early autumn where summers are hot and winters fairly mild. (None do well in Florida, the Gulf coast, and lower Texas.) Plants need regular watering from onset of spring growth until about 6 weeks after bloom has stopped; after that, water established plants only moderately through summer. Divide clumps when they become crowded, about every 3 years. Divide rhizomes (underground stems) with a sharp knife and replant healthy sections with good fan of leaves.

The beardless irises most widely grown are spuria, Louisiana, Siberian, and Japanese. Stiff flowers of spurias resemble the florists' Dutch irises. Colors include white, yellow, and orange shades, brown tones, and light to dark shades of blue and purple. Most have a contrasting yellow spot on the falls. Closely branched flowering stems are 3–5 feet tall, carrying blossoms above narrow, upright leaves.

Louisiana irises tend to have flat flowers; standards and falls are carried in nearly the same plane. Flowers are more graceful than spuria blossoms, and color range is extensive. Flowering stems are branched, 2–5 feet high; leaves are slender but less stiff than spuria foliage.

Siberian irises have fewer colors: white, blue and purple shades and combinations, pink, and wine reds. Graceful, fluttery blossoms are airily poised atop slim stems, 2–4 feet tall. Foliage is almost grassy, in thick clumps.

Japanese irises can be the most spectacular of all for flower size: flat single or double blossoms the size of salad plates. Color range is the same as that of Siberian irises, but with the addition of intricately veined and patterned combinations. Foliage is slender, forming fountainlike clumps.

Three of the four popular beardless irises — Siberian, Louisiana, and Japanese — need soil that is continually moist throughout the growing and blooming season. Louisianas and Japanese irises will grow in the boggy soil of pond or stream margins. Give them neutral to somewhat acid soil (Japanese must have acid soil), in full sun for Siberians, but sun to light shade for Louisianas and Japanese. Louisianas thrive in the humid Gulf coast area as well as in other parts of the country where winter temperature doesn't drop below −10°F/−23°C. Siberians and Japanese are hardy to −35°F/−37°C and are more difficult to grow well in hot-summer/mild-winter regions. Divide plants in late summer to early autumn. Siberians are best in thick, established clumps; Japanese and Louisianas will need dividing more frequently but less often than bearded irises.

Spuria irises need less water than the other beardless types; give them the same treatment as for tall bearded irises. Divide plants in early autumn.

Ivy geranium. See **Pelargonium**

Jacob's ladder. See **Polemonium.**

Japanese anemone. See **Anemone.**

Johnny-jump-up. See **Viola.**

Jupiter's beard. See **Centranthus.**

Kniphofia uvaria

Red-hot poker
Perennial, hardy to −10°F/−23°C
Pictured on page 35

This plant strikes a bold note in the garden. Its thick clumps of coarse grassy foliage, erect or fountainlike, rise 3–4 feet tall. But these bold clumps become more dramatic when 2 feet above the leaves rise flowering spikes bearing "torches" of tubular flowers along the top foot of the spike. Commonly the spikes have yellow flowers at the bottom, and red orange blooms at the top. Modern hybrids include this pattern but also come in cream, yellow, orange, red, pink, and salmon. Two-foot-high dwarfs also are available from some specialists. Bloom season varies from spring through summer.

Plants tolerate considerable heat and some drought but are much better if given moderate to regular watering in well-drained soil. In hottest, driest regions, plant them in part shade, elsewhere in full sun. In areas where winter chill is 0°F/−18°C or below, tie foliage over the clump, then cover protectively.

Lady Washington geranium.
    See **Pelargonium.**

Lamb's ears. See **Stachys.**

Lathyrus

Sweet pea
Annual. Perennial, hardy to −30°F/−34°F
Pictured on page 40

Fresh, dainty, fragrant, and long stemmed, annual sweet peas (*Lathyrus odoratus*) can provide a rainbow of splendid cut flowers in every color but yellow. They grow as vines or bushes from 1–5 feet tall.

In mild-winter regions, plant them in late summer for early-winter flowers, or in early winter for early-spring bloom. In cold-winter areas, sow seeds outdoors in early spring as soon as the ground is dry enough to be worked. For faster germination, soak seeds for several hours before planting, then shake them in a bag with powdered fungicide.

Annual sweet peas grow best in an enriched soil in full sunlight. Screen young plants against birds, and protect them from slugs and snails. Put up a trellis at planting time to support vining types. Water deeply and frequently.

Perennial sweet peas (*L. latifolius*), often seen decorating roadsides, are too attractive to be left out of the garden. Foliage on the strong-growing 6–9 foot vines is soft blue green. Typically, the flowers are light magenta or rosy purple, but there are also kinds with white, rosy red, and pink blooms. Flowering may continue through summer and into autumn if you remove spent blooms.

Start perennial sweet peas from seeds in late winter where winters are mild, in early spring (after the last hard frost) in colder regions. These sweet peas need only average soil and moderate to regular watering. You can grow them on trellises, but they also do well as scrambling mounds fringing a garden or spilling down an embankment.

Lenten rose. See **Helleborus.**

Liatris spicata

Gayfeather
Perennial, hardy to −35°F/−37°C

Linear, fine-textured gayfeather has very narrow, almost grasslike foliage. From clumps of such foliage rise leafy stems to 5 feet high, topped in fluffy, bottlebrush-type spikes of rosy purple or white flowers. Flowers open first at the top of the spike rather than at the base. Blooms come in summer, sometimes extend into early autumn. A dwarf variety is 'Kobold' ('Cobalt'). Nurseries sometimes sell these plants as *L. callilepis.*

The thick, almost tuberous roots need well-drained soil; otherwise they're not too particular. Moderate to regular watering gives best performance, but plants will endure some drought. Divide crowded clumps every 3–4 years in early spring.

Liatris

Lily-of-the-Nile. See **Agapanthus.**

Lily-of-the-Valley. See **Convallaria.**

Lily turf. See **Liriope.**

Limonium

Statice
Annual. Perennial, hardiness varies
Pictured on page 46

Showy garden displays and long-lasting fresh or dried cut flowers are two good reasons for growing statice. Summer-blooming annual statices (*Limonium bonduellii* and *L. sinuatum*) have airy clusters of papery yellow, blue, purple, or rose flowers. The clusters come on much-branched stems that rise up to 2 feet above dense clumps of large and leathery basal leaves.

Sow seeds outdoors in spring in well-drained soil and full sun. Water only moderately — statices do best when kept on the dry side.

Perennial kinds of statice also bloom in summer. They're known as sea lavender because of their ability to tolerate salt-laden seaside air. *Limonium latifolium* (hardy to −30°F/ −34°C) has broad leathery leaves up to 10 inches long. Flowering stems may reach 2½ feet high and the stems from a single clump can spread 3 feet across. Flowers are lavender blue. *Limonium perezii* (hardy to 25°F/ −4°C) can grow up to 3 feet tall. It has wavy-edged leaves, and purple and white blossoms. Both sea lavenders need well-drained soil. Though they're not fussy, they perform best in good soil with regular watering.

Linum

Flax
Annual. Perennial, hardy to −10°F/−23°C; not suited to Gulf coast and Florida
Pictured on page 33

Annual scarlet flax, *L. grandiflorum* 'Rubrum', offers brilliant red, rounded flowers to 1½ inches across on slender, wispy plants. In the garden it still looks like the wildflower that it is, and it will reseed to provide you with plants year after year. Sow seeds in full sun, in autumn or spring, in light, well-drained soil. Plants don't need much water.

Perennial flaxes have similar flowers but in yellow or blue. Golden flax, *L. flavum*, is compact and shrubby, up to 15 inches high except for variety 'Compactum' which is a 6-inch dwarf. Branching clusters bear inch-wide blossoms in spring. Large, white-eyed blue flowers of *L. narbonense* appear from spring into summer on 2-foot plants with slender blue green leaves. Similar, but with smaller blue or white blossoms, is *L. perenne* which blooms from spring to autumn.

The perennial flaxes tend to be short lived, but you can start new plants from cuttings. Plant in full sun, in well-drained, light soil.

Liriope

Lily turf. See Ophiopogon for similar plants
Perennial; hardiness varies

With their neat, evergreen clumps of glossy, grasslike foliage, these plants are popular for borders, small-scale ground cover, and Oriental-style gardens. Liriopes produce flowering stems topped with tight spikes of rounded lavender or white blossoms. In *L. muscari*, hardy to −10°F/−23°C, leaves may be ½ inch wide and up to 2 feet long, forming fountainlike clumps to 18 inches high. Summer flowers may be held just above foliage or partly hidden in it. Several varieties are sold: 'Majestic' is a bit larger and has flowers in cockscomb like clusters; 'Silvery Sunproof' and 'Variegata' have leaves banded with yellow. Creeping lily turf (*L. spicata*, hardy to −20°F/−29°C), spreads by underground stems. Narrower leaves are more lax, making mounds only to about 8 inches high. Established plants look better if cut down annu-

ally in early spring before growth starts.

Filtered sunlight or part shade is best unless summers are cool. Set plants in well-drained soil and give them regular watering for best appearance. Slugs and snails may damage foliage. If you want to increase your planting, dig and divide old clumps in early spring.

Lobelia

Annual. Perennial, hardy to −35°F/−37°C (with winter protection)
Pictured on pages 28, 29

A surprising difference separates annual lobelia from the most familiar perennial species: one is blue and spreading, the other bright red and vertical.

Annual *Lobelia erinus* is a popular edging and container plant. It contributes a Gainsborough-rich palette of blues — sky blue, baby blue, electric blue, sapphire blue. Small tubular, 3-lipped flowers cover branching, spreading plants. Named strains offer different colors of blue (plus white and rose red). Flowers begin in early summer and continue until frost. Give plants well-prepared soil, regular water, full sun where summer is cool, but part shade or filtered sunlight where summer is hot or dry.

Cardinal flower (*L. cardinalis*) grows naturally in moist or boggy soil in the eastern United States and Canada. From rosettes of leaves spring leafy stalks 2–4 feet tall bearing inch-long tubular, bright scarlet blooms, midsummer to autumn.

Sow seeds or set out plants in part shade or filtered sunlight in moist soil. Plants will self sow in the garden if you let seeds ripen. In autumn you can dig and separate new growth from bases of old flowering stems. Protect these transplants over winter; they'll bloom the next summer.

Lobularia maritima

Sweet alyssum
Annual
Pictured on pages 20, 35, 40

In sweet-smelling drifts with a honey-like fragrance, this low, branching plant puts forth clusters of tiny, four-petaled flowers. Blossoms atop its 2–4-inch stalks range from white to shades of rose and violet.

Leaves are ½–2 inches long, narrow or lance shaped.

Sweet alyssum does best in full sun but also tolerates partial shade. Hardy and quick to grow, it requires only ordinary soil, light watering.

In mild-winter climates, broadcast seeds (or set out nursery plants) during spring or fall. After just six weeks, blossoms will appear and will continue to bloom year-round. In colder regions plant seeds in spring, after ground is warm, for bloom until the first autumn frost. Shear plants halfway back, four weeks after blooming starts, to get a new crop of flowers, keep plants less rangy.

Lungwort. See **Pulmonaria**.

Lupine. See **Lupinus**.

Lupinus

Lupine
Perennial, hardy to about −30°F/−34°C
Pictured on page 37

Today's perennial lupines are derived from the Russell hybrids, developed earlier in this century. Typical plant is a bushy clump of attractive foliage. Each leaf is about hand size with many leaflets held like fingers of an outstretched hand. Vertical flower spikes grow to a height of 4–5 feet. Dwarf strains, only 1½ feet high, are Minarette and Little Lulu. Flowers are sweet pea shaped and densely encircle the upright flower spike. Color range is remarkable, including white, cream, yellow, orange, red, pink, purple, blue, and many bicolor combinations. Bloom period is midspring into summer. When a spike has finished flowering, cut it off just above the leaves.

Lupines are successful only where summers are fairly cool: parts of the West Coast, Pacific Northwest, New England, the northern tier of states, and southern Canada. Plant lupines in full sun or filtered sunlight, in a well-drained soil that's neither acid nor alkaline. Set out plants in early spring or raise them from spring-sown seed for bloom the following year. Plants are rather short-lived, and may need to be revitalized or replaced after several years. Division in spring is possible, and new plants can be raised from basal cuttings, but starting over with new plants raised from seed usually is more successful.

Lychnis

Annual. Perennial, hardy to −35°F/−37°C

Pictured on pages 28, 35

Available species differ considerably in appearance, but all offer eye-catching color. Maltese cross (*L. chalcedonica*) produces showy, dense clusters of brilliant scarlet flowers, each about an inch across with 4 cleft petals. Flowers are borne atop 3-foot stems in early summer. A biennial or short-lived perennial, *L. coronaria* reseeds so freely that there is always a supply of fresh plants. Clumps of feltlike gray white leaves send up open, branching flower stems to 2½ feet; each branch bears an inch-wide magenta flower. Bloom is from spring into summer.

L. viscaria (sometimes sold as viscaria) grows from compact clumps of rather grassy foliage. Flowering stems 1–1½ feet high bear upright, open clusters of ½-inch pink, purple, or white blooms in summer.

Lychnis will get along in fairly poor soil as long as it is well drained, and *L. coronaria* will endure infrequent watering. Plant in full sun or lightest shade. *L. viscaria* may need dividing after several years.

Rose-of-heaven (*L. coeli-rosa*), an annual, has single red or white inch-wide flowers on 1–1½-foot-tall plants. Leaves are long, narrow, pointed. Flowers appear during summer, are good for cutting. In spring, sow seeds outdoors in moist soil and full sun.

Lythrum salicaria

Purple loosestrife
Perennial, hardy to −35°F/−37°C; not suited to Gulf coast, Florida

Purple is a bit misleading, as flowers are magenta or rosy red in the basic species, and pink or red shades in named hybrids. Plants make clumps of upright, leafy stems, with narrow, pointed leaves. In summer and into early autumn, the upper 18 inches of the 3–5-foot stems become spikes of 1-inch, closely set flowers.

In the garden, purple loosestrife thrives in damp soil but does well in good garden soil with ordinary watering—in sun or part shade. Remove spent flower spikes to prevent abundant self sowing. Clumps may remain in place for many years.

M

Madagascar periwinkle. See **Catharanthus.**

Maiden pink. See **Dianthus**

Maltese cross. See **Lychnis.**

Marguerite. See **Chrysanthemum.**

Marigold. See **Tagetes.**

Martha Washington geranium. See **Pelargonium.**

Matthiola

Stock
Annual

Pictured on page 40

Called "gilliflower" in George Washington's day, stock has long been a favorite of American gardeners. Its fluffy spikes of single or double blossoms, crowning 1–3-foot stems, make elegant cut flowers that carry a unique, spicy perfume. Flowers are in shades of lavender, magenta, pink, purple, rose, yellow, and white.

Grow stock from seeds or nursery plants. Choose a type suited for your climate; Giant Imperial and Column types are recommended only for mild-winter climates. In late autumn, sow seeds directly in the garden for spring bloom. In mild or cold areas, you can successfully grow Dwarf Ten Weeks stock and Trysomic Seven Weeks strain. Sow seed thickly, very early in spring. Don't try to force early blooming by thinning or fertilizing young plants.

Stock likes a sunny location with light, fertile, well-drained soil, though it will tolerate partial shade. Water regularly.

Meadow rue. See **Thalictrum.**

Meadow sweet. See **Astilbe.**

Mexican sunflower. See **Tithonia.**

Michaelmas daisies. See **Aster.**

Mignonette. See **Reseda.**

Mimulus hybridus

Monkey flower
Perennial; grown as annual

Pictured on page 53

When in bloom, monkey flower boasts a profusion of 2½-inch flowers brilliantly colored in gold, red, or yellow, and sometimes strikingly mottled with brown or maroon. A small

---

plant for the size of its blossoms, it thrives at the shaded edge of a pool, or where the soil is moist and ferns or violets do well. It is an excellent potted plant, and, in cool rooms, its cut flowers last 3–4 days. Plants grow 1–2½ feet tall, most types with long, slightly sticky, toothed leaves.

Mimulus is rather touchy. It wants coolness and moist soil, and needs protection from direct sunlight; it doesn't do well in heavy shade.

Start seeds indoors in winter in 8-inch pots. Take the small plants outdoors, sinking their pots into he soil when danger of frost is past. In containers, mimulus will need frequent feeding and watering, but in autumn you can bring them indoors for winter bloom.

Mirabilis jalapa

Four o'clock
Perennial; grown as annual in cold-winter climates

Pictured on page 55

When it comes to blooming, four o'clocks are truly late sleepers. They wait until midsummer to bloom and then continue through autumn, and, as their common name suggests, they keep their flowers shut tight until late afternoon, unless the day is cloudy. Nonetheless, the plants' dense, dark green foliage and profusion of trumpet-shaped flowers act as refreshers in flower gardens that may be past their prime in autumn. Flower colors include white, pink, salmon, lavender, to yellow.

Four o'clocks grow 3–4 feet high in one summer and spread as much as 3 feet. They're especially popular in urban communities because they're hardly affected by excess dust, fumes, and soot. Just hose them off and they're fine.

Plants grow fast from seeds scattered in open, sunny places where the soil is warm and all frost is past.

Moluccella

Bells-of-Ireland
Annual

Pictured on page 47

In graceful spires, bell-shaped sepals resembling large green flowers surround tiny, scented white flowers on this most unusual plant. Willowy stems grow 1½–3 feet tall, arching

---

slightly under the weight of the "bells" along their length. With leaves removed, flower spikes are attractive when dried; they turn creamy-gold.

In short-summer climates, start seeds indoors in flats. Otherwise, sow seeds outside in well-drained soil that gets plenty of sun in early spring. Seeds are slow to germinate unless chilled. If weather is warm, store seeds in refrigerator for a week before sowing. Water frequently and fertilize plants during the growing season.

Mondo grass. See **Ophiopogon**.

Monkey flower. See **Mimulus**.

Monkshood. See **Aconitum**.

Moonflower. See **Ipomoea**.

Morning glory.
See **Convolvulus, Ipomoea**.

Mountain bluet. See **Centaurea**.

Mullein. See **Verbascum**.

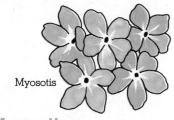
Myosotis

Myosotis

Forget-me-not. See also Anchusa
Annual. Perennial, hardy to −35°F/−37°C

Whether annual or perennial, forget-me-nots feature tiny yellow-centered blue flowers in loose clusters. The annual species, *M. sylvatica* (sometimes sold as *M. alpestris*) reseeds so prolifically that once it's in the garden it seems to be perennial. It grows about a foot high with softly hairy, 2-inch oval leaves. Bloom begins in late winter or earliest spring (depending on climate) and continues until summer or hot weather arrives.

Perennial forget-me-not (*M. scorpioides*) is lower, with bright green glossy leaves; it is spreading in habit. *M. s. semperflorens* blooms throughout summer.

Part shade and plenty of water suit both species (perennial forget-me-not will thrive on a moist stream bank). Both are useful as ground covers in semishade and in wood-land plantings. Summer is the time to divide or move the perennial species.

Nasturtium. See **Tropaeolum**.

Nemesia strumosa

Nemesia
Annual
Pictured on pages 20, 28, 29, 38

A cool-weather annual with delicate and brilliant flowers massed on short bushy plants, nemesia blooms from early summer until heat kills it off. Its ¾-inch flowers appear in every color but green.

In mild-winter climates, plant nemesia outdoors in full sun in autumn or very early spring; elsewhere, plant nemesia outdoors only after danger of frost is past. Keep soil moist but not soggy, and apply fertilizer regularly to established plants.

Nemophila

Baby blue eyes
Annual
Pictured on page 33

In spring, baby blue eyes bears masses of clear, sky-blue flowers with white centers and cupped petals. The 1–1½-inch blooms top fragile stems that grow 6–10 inches tall, putting forth dainty leaves with rounded lobes. Attractive in hanging baskets, baby-blue-eyes also looks lovely in drifts with daffodils or tulips, or as an edging for other cool-loving and quick-blooming annuals. Cut flowers last 2–3 days.

Sow seeds in autumn or early spring. Scatter seeds thickly in moist soil that receives afternoon shade. Set nursery plants close enough so that their foliage will shade the soil.

Nepeta faassenii

Catmint
Perennial, hardy to −35°F/−37°C; not suited to Gulf coast and Florida
Pictured on pages 18, 34

At the edge of a sunny path, catmint will give a lavish show of lavender blue in early summer. Plants are informally spreading, about a foot high, and clothed in aromatic gray green foliage—each leaf a textured 1-inch oval. Flowering spikes rise to 1½–2 feet bearing loose clusters of many small blossoms. If you shear off spent flower spikes, a second burst of bloom may follow. Like its close relative catnip (*N. cataria*), this plant is attractive to cats. Some nurseries sell it as *N. mussinii*.

Catmint needs well-drained soil, full sun, and just moderate watering.

Nicotiana

Flowering tobacco
Perennial; grown as annual
Pictured on page 19

Old-fashioned fragrance gardens wouldn't have been complete without flowering tobacco plants. Those sweet-scented plants opened and released their fragrance in the evening or on cloudy days. Now, flowering tobacco plants have been bred to bloom all day in a wider range of colors: lime, mauve, maroon, pink, red, white. The trumpet-shaped flowers are borne on 1–3-foot-tall stems with large fuzzy leaves at the bases.

Sow seeds or set out plants in spring. Sow seeds directly in the garden when the soil has warmed up, or start them indoors 6–8 weeks before you plan to set them out. Plants need good soil and full sun, except in the hottest areas where they need partial shade. Give plants ample water.

Nierembergia

Cup flower
Perennial, hardiness varies
Pictured on pages 18, 55

Blossoms about an inch across are 5-petaled, wide-open to nearly flat bells. Two kinds are shrubby, with narrow leaves less than an inch long, and hardy only to 15°F/−9°C. Of these, *N. hippomanica violacea* (*N. h. caerulea*) grows in a spreading mound 6–12 inches high, covered with violet blue flowers in summer. Taller, to 3 feet, is *N. scoparia* (*N. frutescens*), with summer flowers of blue-tinted white. Both can be grown as annuals in colder climates. A bit hardier, to 5°F/−15°C is *N. repens* (*N. rivularis*) which displays its white flowers on ground-covering plants with oval, bright green leaves.

Plant cup flowers in full sun where summers are cool, in filtered sun where hot and dry. Give them well-prepared soil and regular watering.

Obedient plant. See **Physostegia.**

Oenothera

Evening primrose, Sundrop
Perennial, hardy to −30°F/−34°C

Sundrops offer cheery yellow, broadly cup-shaped flowers of four silky petals. Ozark sundrop, *O. missourensis*, forms a sprawling plant with stems that turn upward to about 9 inches, with narrow, velvety leaves to 5 inches long. Flowers are surprisingly large for the plant: 3–5 inches across, primarily in summer. Shrubbier, to 2 feet high, *O. tetragona* has smaller, broader, shiny foliage, and flowers about 1½ inches across; stems and buds are reddish brown. Plants sold as *O. fruticosa* and 'Youngii' are this species.

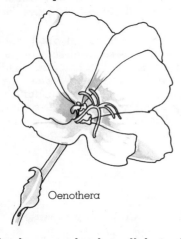

Oenothera

Sundrops need only well-drained soil and moderate watering. Plant in full sun. If plantings become crowded, divide in autumn in milder regions, early spring elsewhere.

Old woman. See **Artemisia.**

Ophiopogon

See also Liriope
Perennial, hardy to 15°F/−9°C

These plants are like *Liriopes* (see page 83). One of them, *O. jaburan*, is sometimes sold as *Liriope gigantea*. All have shiny, narrow to grasslike foliage. Largest leaves are on *O. jaburan*: as much as 3 feet long and ½ inch wide. Plants form dense, rather floppy clumps that bear clusters of small, nodding white flowers, partly hidden in the foliage, in summer. These are followed by round, metallic blue fruit.

A form with leaves striped in white is *O. j.* 'Vittatus', but it may be the same as *Liriope muscari* 'Variegata'. Mondo grass, *O. japonicus*, is a familiar ground cover, forming dense, fountainlike clumps but also spreading by underground runners. The very narrow leaves are up to a foot long, and the spikes of lavender flowers (also followed by blue fruit) are mostly hidden by the leaves. An exotic curiosity is *O. planiscapus* 'Arabicus'. The arching 10-inch leaves emerge green but quickly turn black; loose spikes of summer flowers are pinkish white.

Plants do best in filtered sunlight or part shade. Where summers are cool, they grow in sunny spots. Give them well-drained soil and regular watering. They'll endure some drought, but at the expense of good growth and looks. Slugs and snails may disfigure foliage.

Oriental poppy. See **Papaver.**

Osteospermum

African daisy
Perennial, hardy to 20°F/−7°C
Pictured on page 59

Gardeners in the West can enjoy the long-season bloom of these South African natives. One is a popular ground cover, the rest are shrubby. All have medium-green foliage, generally oval but rather variable in size and shape, with long-stemmed, flat, usually dark-centered daisies.

Trailing African daisy, *O. fruticosum* (sometimes sold as *Dimorphotheca fruticosa*), is the ground cover. Growing to 12 inches high, it spreads rapidly, rooting along branches; one new plant may cover a 4-foot circle of ground in one year. The 2-inch flowers are generally lilac white with purple centers, but there are selected forms in white and deep purple. Blooms come sporadically all year, but main season is winter. It's an excellent seashore plant.

Shrubby kinds need pinching back when young to encourage bushiness; mature plants may need straggling stems cut back to restore shape. *O. barberae (Dimorphotheca barberae)* grows in a flattened mound to 3 feet tall; 2–3-inch flowers are lilac pink with dark bluish centers, and darker stripes on petal backs. Flowering normally goes from autumn through spring, possibly into summer as well. *O. ecklonis (Dimorphotheca ecklonis)* grows to 4 feet high and wide; it flowers from early summer until autumn frost. White blossoms with dark blue centers are tinted blue on petal backs.

Set out plants in full sun in good soil. Regular watering is best though they'll survive with less. For new plants, take cuttings in summer.

Paeonia

Peony
Perennial, hardy to −40°F/−40°C; needs winter temperatures below 32°F/0°C
Pictured on page 49

Herbacous peonies are cherished for their spectacular late-spring blossoms that divert attention from the beauty of their foliage. Each spring, new shoots rise from below the ground and develop into rounded, shrublike clumps (to 4 feet high) of beautiful large leaves divided into numerous segments. From round buds at tips of stems come the impressive blossoms: silk or satin-textured, fully double (like pompons), semidouble, or single (with a fluff of yellow stamenodes in Japanese types), and up to 10 inches across. Peony specialists list countless named varieties in white, pink shades, red shades (including brownish and chocolate reds), even cream and light yellow.

Where winter cold can't be counted upon, a peony's performance will be variable. In such regions, the nearly single Japanese types will consistently perform better. A well-planted, well-located peony can remain undisturbed indefinitely. Turn soil deeply, with plenty of organic matter, in advance of the usual late summer or early autumn planting period. (In some parts of the West, peony roots are available in earliest spring.) Planting depth is critical: position the growth buds ("eyes") at the top of the roots) 1½ inches below soil surface. Planted too deep, peonies will not flower.

Full sun is best, in a location sheltered from strong winds that can topple the heavy blooms. Where spring bloom season is dry and hot, choose earliest flowering varieties and plant where shaded in afternoon. Double-flowered varieties may need staking to remain upright.

Botrytis blight sometimes is a problem. Flower buds turn brown, fail to open, and foliage and stems become brown-spotted. Cut off and destroy infected parts, spray plants with benomyl, then spray again the following spring before buds show color.

Painted daisy. See **Chrysanthemum.**

Painted-tongue. See **Salpiglossis.**

Pansy. See **Viola.**

Papaver

Poppy
Annual. Perennial, hardiness varies
Pictured on pages 20, 32, 45, and 48

All poppies possess cup-shaped blossoms of shimmering, silky texture. Annual Shirley poppies are a strain developed from *P. rhoeas*, the famous red 'corn poppy' of Flanders fields. Flowering plants may be 2–5 feet tall. In addition to red, colors include pink shades, orange, and bicolor flowers, both single and double. Plants are slender, with hairy stems and divided leaves.

In late autumn, mix tiny seeds with fine sand and sow in the garden as you would wildflowers (see page 32). In colder regions, seeds will germinate in spring and bloom in late spring and summer. In milder areas, seeds will germinate in winter and start blooming in late winter or early spring.

Iceland poppy (*P. nudicaule*) is a perennial that's usually grown as an annual. From clumps of hairy, finely divided leaves rise 1–2-foot knitting-needle stalks, each topped by one satiny flower about 3 inches wide. Colors run the gamut of warm pastel shades, orange, yellow, deep pink, and white. Sow seeds as for Shirley poppies (above) or set out nursery plants. These are cool-season flowers: winter or spring bloom in mild climates, early summer bloom in cold-winter areas.

The reliable perennial Oriental poppy (*P. orientale*), is the monarch of the group. Great bowl-shaped blossoms, occasionally up to a foot wide, command notice. Clumps of finely divided, very hairy leaves send up leafy flower stalks 2–4 feet high in midspring. The original forms had neon-bright orange blooms with black centers, but among the many named hybrids are many colors. Tall varieties may need staking. Foliage dies back soon after flowering; roots send up new growth again in early autumn. Plants must have well-drained soil and a climate that gives some winter chilling below 32°F/0°C. Late summer to early autumn is the time to plant or divide the fleshy roots. Set plant crowns about 3 inches below soil surface.

All poppies prefer soil that is well-drained and not too rich. Plant in full sun and water moderately.

Parma violet. See **Viola.**

Pelargonium

Geranium
Perennial, hardy to 28°F/−2°C
Pictured on front cover and pages 21, 29

Though their use as perennials is limited to frost-free and nearly frost-free areas, these various geraniums can be grown as annuals anywhere and are favorite container plants. In cold regions, potted plants can be overwintered indoors or in a greenhouse. The familiar showy sorts are Martha Washington geraniums or pelargoniums (*P. domesticum*), common geranium (*P. hortorum*), and ivy geranium (*P. peltatum*).

Martha Washington types are shrubby, to 3 feet or more, with rounded to heart-shaped leaves (to 4 inches across), that have fluted edges. Rounded, ruffly flowers are in clusters, each bloom to 2 inches wide, in spring and summer. Colors include white, pink, red, purple, and lavender shades, often with dark, velvety blotches on some petals.

Common geraniums also are shrubby and about the same size, but with soft hairy leaves and stems. Individual flowers (single or double) are smaller, but clusters may be larger and fuller than Martha Washington types. Colors are white, pink, salmon, orange, red, purple.

Ivy geraniums are trailing plants used as ground covers, or in contain-

ers where they can spill over the edges. Leaves are thick, glossy, resembling ivy. Moderate-size clusters of 1-inch flowers (single or double) may be white, lavender, pink shades, red. There are varieties with variegated foliage.

Scented geraniums, also pelargonium species, are grown mostly for leaf fragrance. Aromas include lemon, lime, apple, rose, and peppermint.

Pelargoniums are nearly succulents. Give them light, well-drained soil and moderate watering; let soil dry to about an inch deep, then water thoroughly. Be sure to water potted plants regularly. Where summers are hot — especially hot and dry — give plants light shade, filtered sunlight, or shade during hottest part of the day. To promote bushiness, pinch out growing tips periodically. In climates where they will persist as perennials, prune plants back to at least half their size in late winter or early spring, just as growing season begins. Potential pests are tobacco budworm, aphids, and spider mites.

Penstemon

Beard tongue
Perennial, hardiness varies
Pictured on page 54

Penstemons have tubular to trumpet-shaped flowers, often in bright colors and carried in loose spikes at ends of stems; leaves are narrow and pointed. Hardiest — to −35°F/−37°C, and needing sub-freezing winters to perform — is *P. barbatus*. This branching, somewhat sprawling plant bears 1-inch red flowers. Several named selections are sold: 'Prairie Dusk' (purple), 'Prairie Fire' (scarlet), and 'Rose Elf'; these grow 18–30 inches tall. The largest flowers are found in *P. gloxinioides*: 2-inch trumpets (on 2–3-foot stems) in various shades of pink and red, often with white throats. Plants are hardy to 0°F/−18°C or a bit lower, but can be grown as summer-flowering annuals in colder aeas. Spring-flowering *P. heterophyllus purdyi* may vary from lilac to intense blue, but the form 'Blue Bedder' usually is a good bright blue. Plants are both upright and sprawling, ranging from 12–24 inches high.

Well-drained soil is a necessity, especially soil that's not soggy in winter. Given good drainage, plants appreciate regular watering. Locate them in sun, but in filtered sunlight or partial shade where summers are hot. Plants are fairly short-lived (4 years) but replacement plants are easily started from cuttings.

Peony. See **Paeonia.**

Persian cornflower. See **Centaurea.**

Peruvian lily. See **Alstroemeria.**

Petunia hybrida

Tender perennial; grown as annual
Pictured on pages 19, 31, 38

Highly popular, petunias rank with marigolds and zinnias as sun-loving garden favorites. Their popularity is well deserved. Their abundant trumpet-shaped single or double blossoms have a pleasant fragrance and offer a banquet of colors. Petunias thrive in almost all temperate climates. They're good bedding plants and container plants, either by themselves or in combination with other plants. Of the two general classes, Grandifloras have large flowers, Multifloras have more but smaller flowers. Petunias are used mostly for summer color. (In mild parts of the West, they are planted in autumn for late winter and early spring bloom.)

To start petunias from seeds, sow them in flats or in the open ground when the soil has warmed in spring. Mix tiny seeds with sand to get even spreading. Because they take a little more time to flower from seed than most annuals, start them about 10 weeks before the last frost date for your area.

For a quicker start, set out seedlings from a nursery when weather is warm. Petunias need good, well-drained soil and full sun. Give them ample water, and fertilize plants about once a month. If tobacco budworm troubles your plants, see "Pests & Diseases," page 15.

Phlox

Annual. Perennial, hardy to −30°F/−34°–C
Pictured on pages 17, 25, 61

Summer is phlox time—in fact, generations of gardeners have considered summer incomplete without them. Their colors, in light through dark tones, range from red through

violet, plus white. Flowers are circular in outline, with 5 petals often overlapping. Blooms may be small, but are showy in dense clusters.

Annual phlox *(P. drummondii)* is available in various strains from 6–8 inches tall. Low kinds are fine as edging plants and small-scale ground cover; taller ones are colorful foreground and filler plants. Set out plants in spring where winters are cold, in autumn where summers are hot and winters mild.

Perennial sorts range from ground covers to the 4-foot spectaculars. Sweet William phlox *(P. divaricata)* has loose clusters of bluish blooms that appear in spring. The foot-high plants spread by underground stems. A good blue is *P. d. laphamii;* there is a white-flowered form.

Beginning in early summer is 3–4-foot *P. carolina* (sometimes sold as *P. suffruticosa).* Shiny, lance-shaped leaves rise up the stems which are topped by cylindrical flower clusters to 15 inches long. Typical color is magenta pink, but a good white selection is 'Miss Lingard.' Foliage is free of pests and diseases that can bother summer phlox.

At their peak in midsummer are the many named forms of summer phlox *(P. paniculata),* though some will begin blooming earlier and many will continue through summer into autumn. Blooms come in dome-shaped clusters atop leafy stems that may be 2½–4 feet or more in height. Colors include white, lavender through purple, pink through red, salmon orange — many with a contrasting spot of color in the center of each flower.

Perennial phloxes grow best in a well-drained rich soil. Sweet William phlox prefers light shade or filtered sunlight; the other kinds are best in sun. All need regular watering. Leaves of summer phlox are subject to mildew so avoid overhead watering and crowding plants close together or next to walls or hedges that reduce air circulation. Summer phlox and *P. carolina* need dividing every 3–4 years to restore vigor.

Physostegia virginiana

False dragonhead, Obedient plant
Perennial, hardy to −35°F/−37°C
Pictured on page 63

Flower appearance is somewhat like foxglove and snapdragon. Like them,

the flowers of false dragonhead are carried in spikes. Each flower, if twisted or pushed out of position, will remain in place, hence the name "obedient plant." Spreading clumps send up stems of toothed, lance-shaped leaves to 5 inches long. At late-summer bloom season, stems may reach 4 feet, the top 1–1½ feet bearing blossoms. Basic color is bright bluish pink, but there are named selections in rose pink and white. Some named kinds grow only 2 or 3 feet high.

These plants thrive in full sun and good soil, and with plenty of moisture. Under those conditions they tend to spread rapidly and need dividing and thinning about every other year. Do this in early spring.

Pincushion flower. See **Scabiosa.**

Pink. See **Dianthus.**

Plantain lily. See **Hosta.**

Platycodon

Platycodon grandiflorus

Balloon flower
Perennial, hardy to −35°F/−37°C; not suited to Gulf coast and Florida

Flowers like wide open, star-shaped campanulas bloom from nearly-round buds that can be popped open with thumb-and-forefinger pressure — hence the name "balloon flower." Plants are upright, to about 3 feet, and bushy with oval, 3-inch, olive green leaves. Bloom begins in early summer and will continue for 2 months or more if you remove spent blossoms individually. The basic color is violet blue, but there are selected forms with flowers of white and pink, and there is a double-flowered blue variant. *P. g. mariesii* is no more than 18 inches tall.

Best conditions are a well-prepared, fairly light, well-drained soil. Plant in light shade or filtered sunlight where summers are hot; otherwise in full sun. Give moderate watering. Plants break dormancy late, after most other perennials.

Polemonium

Perennial, hardy to −35°F/−37°C; not for mild-winter/hot-summer areas

Fernlike, feathery leaves give the name "Jacob's ladder" to at least one of these plants, *P. caeruleum*. From foliage clumps rise stems to 2 feet high bearing loose clusters of somewhat bell-shaped and nodding lavender blue flowers; there's also a white-flowered form. About half as high, and spreading, is *P. reptans*, usually available in the variety 'Blue Pearl' (often sold as *P. c.* 'Blue Pearl'). Flowering is midspring into summer.

Good soil, regular watering, and part shade spell success for polemoniums. Plants will need dividing after several years; do this in early spring, or early autumn.

Poppy. See **Papaver.**

Portulaca grandiflora

Rose moss
Annual
Pictured on page 50

Portulaca is a good temporary ground cover for rock gardens or driveway strips. Looking like single or double roses, its vivid, 2-inch-wide flowers come in lavender, magenta, orange, red, white, and yellow. They're profusely borne on succulent plants only 6 inches high, but up to 18 inches wide.

Heat tolerant and drought resistant, portulaca thrives where summers are long and hot, but does well where summers are cool and short.

Plant seeds in warm well-drained soil and full sun after danger of frost is past. Since seeds are very fine, mix them with sand and sprinkle in rows spaced 14 inches apart; or scatter over an area as a ground cover. Press soil down firmly; seeds will find their

own spot, but won't germinate if buried too deep. Keep soil moist until seeds sprout. Once established, plants get along fine with light watering. For early bloom, start seeds indoors at 70°–75°F/21°–24°C about 2 months before date of last expected frost; they will sprout in 7–10 days.

Pot marigold. See **Calendula.**

Primrose. See **Primula.**

Primula

Primrose
Perennial, hardiness varies
Pictured on page 20, 39

Literally hundreds of primrose species exist, but only a few kinds are widely sold. (Many of the rarer kinds are sold by specialists.) All form rosettes of leaves above which the circular flowers are borne on individual stems, in clusters at ends of stems, or in tiered clusters up the stems. Flowering season ranges from winter through spring, depending on the species.

The most familiar plant in nurseries is *P. polyantha* (hardy to −30°F/−34°C). Its tongue-shaped leaves grow about 8 inches long and resemble romaine lettuce. Above them on 6–12-inch stems are clusters of 1–2-inch flowers in a dazzling range of colors, from soft to bright, in everything but green, each flower with pronounced yellow center. Two other species, hardy to −20°F/−29°C, are similar but smaller. Cowslip (*P. veris*) produces nodding clusters of fragrant yellow flowers in early spring. It's more demanding of "primrose conditions" (see below) than *P. polyantha*. Another similar and less widely adapted species is the English primrose (*P. vulgaris*). Early spring flowers come singly on a stem or in groups of 2 or 3; colors include red, blue, yellow, white, and brownish shades, and there are double-flowered varieties.

Hybrids of *P. juliae*, hardy to −20°F/−29°C, form low tufts of foliage that is nearly covered with flowers in early spring, again in a wide range of colors. These enjoy woodland conditions and are not for warm-winter regions. Also needing winter chill to about −20°F/−29°C is *P. denticulata*. Its leaves resemble those of *P. polyantha*, but they are only about half their mature size when bloom occurs in early spring. Flowers are in

dense, ball-shaped clusters atop foot-high stems. Differing from these in several respects is fairy primrose (*P. malacoides*), hardy to 25°F/−4°C. Though a perennial, it's usually grown as an annual and thrives in mild-winter regions. Leaves are oval, lobed, on long stalks. The small flowers are carried in airy, tiered clusters on stems to 15 inches tall. Bloom is from midwinter into spring.

Primroses originated in moist meadows and woodlands, in climates that often are cool and humid. These are, of course, the ideal conditions for most primroses. Soil should be well-enriched with organic matter and well drained, but not allowed to go dry. Part shade or dappled sunlight usually is best, although *P. polyantha* will take sun where summers are cool or frequently overcast or foggy. Crowded clumps can be divided right after flowering.

Pulmonaria

Lungwort
Perennial, hardy to −35°F/−37°C; not suited to mild-winter/hot-summer areas

Not spectacular, but charming, pulmonarias bring soft spring color to shaded and moist gardens. Flowers are funnel or trumpet shaped; in clusters, they nod atop short stems. Lance-shaped, hairy leaves may reach 6 inches long and grow in clumps; flowering stems also bear leaves.

Blue lungwort (*P. angustifolia*) may reach 12 inches high. Typically it has blue flowers that open from pink buds, but plants raised from seed may vary considerably. A bright blue form may be sold as *P. a. azurea*, and there is a pale yellow sold as 'Lutea.' Leaves spotted with near-white distinguish Bethlehem sage (*P. saccharata*); plant is taller (to about 18 inches) and bears flowers of pink, blue violet, or white.

Moist but well-drained soil is preferred, and plants will thrive in shade (fern conditions). They can be used as a limited ground cover, especially under deciduous trees and shrubs. In time, crowded clumps will need dividing; do this in early autumn and keep newly set plants well watered.

Purple coneflower. See **Echinacea.**

Purple loosestrife. See **Lythrum.**

R

Rainbow pink. See **Dianthus.**

Red-hot poker. See **Kniphofia.**

Red valerian. See **Centranthus.**

Reseda odorata

Mignonette
Annual

Mignonette is the quintessence of nosegays. Its fragrance is sublime, impossible to describe with justice, though "sweet" and "clean" come close. Among pale green foliage, the tiny yellow and white blossoms cluster in spikes 12–18 inches high. The plant has sprawling growth habits and a rather weedy appearance, as if it focused all its refinement on its fragrance. The most perfumed varieties are 'Common Sweet Scented' and 'Machet.' Cut flowers last for a week or more.

Sow mignonette seeds outdoors in warm soil. Successive sowings every three weeks will assure your garden of fragrance throughout the summer. (Plant beneath a frequently opened window, so the fragrance can drift indoors.)

Mignonette grows quickly. It prefers full sun, but tolerates partial shade. In mild climates, it blooms from spring through autumn, but extremely hot weather may dry up the flowers.

Rose-mallow. See **Hibiscus.**

Rose moss. See **Portulaca.**

Rudbeckia

Gloriosa daisy, Black-eyed Susan
Perennial, hardy to −35°F/−37°C
Pictured on pages 17, 38, 55

The wild forms of these sunny daisies — black-eyed-Susan, coneflower, and golden glow—may be familiar in many parts of the country as field and roadside plants. But these often rangy and rampant wildflowers have been subdued by plant breeders for garden ornament. Common names stem from their typically dark centers that usually are a cone shape.

Gloriosa daisy or black-eyed Susan (*R. hirta*), a fairly short-lived perennial, has named strains. Its 4-inch blooms range from yellow through mahogany, sometimes bicolored; and there are doubles. Rough, pointed-oval leaves form vigorous clumps that send up 3–4-foot stems in summer and into fall. *R. fulgida* 'Goldsturm' produces single, yellow, dark-centered flowers on 2-foot stems in summer and fall. Towering 6–7 feet is golden glow, *R. laciniata* 'Hortensia', with light green leaves deeply lobed and bright yellow double flowers. More useful in the average garden is the variety 'Goldquelle' reaching a bushy 2½ feet high.

Abundant bloom over a long period comes with little fussing. Give rudbeckias full sun, average soil, and moderate watering. Clumps may need dividing in 2–3 years; early spring is the best time.

S

Sage. See **Salvia.**

Salpiglossis sinuata

Painted-tongue
Annual
Pictured on page 42

Cousin to the more widely acclaimed petunia, salpiglossis is prized for exceptionally rich colors and curious markings. Excellent as cut flowers, the 2–3-inch trumpet-shaped blooms glow gold, mahogany, red-orange, scarlet and purple. Many are further embellished with pencil-fine tracings of contrasting colors. All this artistic glory reaches a height of 2–3 feet.

Salpiglossis is somewhat difficult to start from seeds. The best way is to put several seeds in peat pots filled with potting mix during late winter or early spring. Keep the mix moist and the pots in a warm, protected dark spot. After seeds sprout (in 7–10 days), move them into a warm, lighted place, and thin to one seedling per pot. Transplant outdoors after seedlings are well established and all danger of frost is past. Choose a sunny location with rich soil and protection from wind. Plants need generous water in the beginning, but less as they grow. Weak, slender stems may need propping.

Salvia

Sage, Scarlet sage
Annual. Perennial, hardiness varies
Pictured on pages 21, 30, 38

Flower-laden spires of dazzling red, rising from dark green foliage, make annual scarlet sage (*Salvia splendens*) a bright exclamation point in your garden. Take care where you use it, for its vibrant red will often overpower more tepid garden colors. Though red shades are most common, you can also find scarlet sage in pink, deep purple, and white. Plants grow from 8–30 inches high.

Scarlet sage is somewhat slow to germinate from seeds. Start them indoors in a warm sunny spot 8 weeks before the last spring-frost date (page 7). Transplant seedlings after soil warms. Or, you may prefer to buy flats of vigorous young plants from a nursery.

Scarlet sage thrives in full sun, but can stand partial shade. Expect a blaze of color from June until frost.

Most perennial salvias bear small tubular flowers in penetrating shades of blue and violet massed together in spikes at branch tips. A bushy plant about 5 feet high, *S. azurea grandiflora* (*Salvia pitcheri*) has narrow, pointed green leaves and brilliant blue flowers from midsummer into autumn. Hardiness is to −20°F/−29°C. Bushy, about 3 feet tall, *Salvia farinacea* has gray green foliage and blue violet flowers in late summer and autumn; plant is hardy to 10°F/−12°C, but can be grown as an annual in colder regions. The same is true of *Salvia patens*. It forms a mounding 2-foot plant with arrow-shaped green leaves and 2-inch dark blue flowers from summer into autumn. *Salvia pratensis* (*S. haematodes*) grows as a rosette of dark green, wavy leaves; from this come much-branched 3½-foot stems of lavender blue blossoms in early summer. Plants are hardy to −20°F/−29°C. *Salvia superba* is a greenleafed, compact plant about 2½ feet high, usually available in its shorter (1½–2 feet) selection, 'Ostfriesland', which produces many upright, vibrant violet blue flower spikes beginning in early summer.

These perennial salvias prefer sun in good, definitely well-drained soil. Moderate watering is sufficient. Crowded clumps may need dividing after a few years, in early spring.

Scabiosa

Pincushion flower
Annual. Perennial, hardy to −30°F/−34°C

A sprinkling of protruding stamens looking like pins in a cushion give this lofty, exotic flower its name. Annual *Scabiosa atropurpurea* (usually sold as *S. grandiflora*), grows 2–4 feet high and bears 2-inch-wide multi-rayed, dome-shaped blossoms throughout the summer. Colors range from white through blues and reds to maroon.

Easy to grow, pincushion flower thrives wherever summers are not extremely hot. Sow seeds in warm soil and full sun where plants are to remain. Massed together, plants look less spindly, and their heavy flowers are less likely to droop. Pinching off stem tips encourages bushier growth. Remove flowers as they fade.

A readily available perennial scabiosa is *S. caucasica*. Typical flowers are lavender blue or white on 2–2½-foot stems during summer. Plant in full sun, in soil that is well drained and not acid. Best performance is where summers are neither hot nor dry. For hot areas, the similar *S. columbaria* is a better choice.

Scarlet flax. See **Linum**.

Scarlet sage. See **Salvia**.

Schizanthus pinnatus

Butterfly flower
Annual
Pictured on page 29

Clouds of tiny orchidlike blossoms in shades of pink, rose, lilac, purple, and white—all with yellow throats— are the reward of growing butterfly flowers. Plants, covered with ferny foliage, grow up to 1½ feet tall. They bloom in summer in most areas, or in late winter and early spring where winters are mild. These showy plants are wonderful combined in containers with other annuals, or planted with cinerarias and *Primula malacoides*. Like these plants, they do best when the weather is cool.

Sow seeds indoors about 4 weeks before planting time. Set them out in rich, moist soil in filtered shade and give ample water.

Sea lavender. See **Limonium**

Sedum

Stonecrop
Perennial, hardy to −35°F/−37°C

The larger sedums spend spring and summer as increasingly taller clumps of handsome foliage with fleshy, oval, scallop-edged leaves in tones that vary from gray green to bronze. Flowering occurs in late summer, extends into autumn. Individual blooms are tiny stars and are grouped together into showy, flat-topped clusters.

S. maximum 'Atropurpureum' grows to 2 feet high. It has bronze purple stems and leaves, and creamy pink flowers. Most widely sold is *S. spectabile*, up to 18 inches tall and pink flowered in the typical form. Selected forms are 'Brilliant' (rose red), 'Carmen' (soft rose), 'Meteor' (carmine red), and 'Star Dust' (ivory). Similar, but with narrower leaves and inclined to be taller, is *S. telephium*. Its variety, 'Autumn Joy,' has coppery pink flowers that become rusty brown red as they age.

Best growth is in full sun in good well-drained soil with routine watering, but sedums will take poorer soil and some neglect. In time, clumps become crowded and need dividing in early spring.

Senecio

Cineraria, Dusty miller
Perennial (some treated as annual); hardiness varies
Pictured on page 57

In the cool shade where cinerarias *(Senecio hybridus)* thrive, their daisy-like flowers sparkle in light to dark shades of blue, magenta, pink, purple, and shining white.

A tender perennial that's mostly grown as an annual, cineraria is often sold in pots in full bloom. Large-flowered strains, with blooms 3–5 inches wide in big, compact clusters of mixed colors, are most popular. They grow 12–15 inches high and have large attractive heart-shaped leaves. Cinerarias bloom in late winter and early spring in mild-winter areas, and from spring to early summer where winters are cold.

Set out plants in cool shaded areas in rich, well-drained soil after spring frost is past. Water frequently to keep soil moist, but don't let it get soggy.

Container-grown plants need fertilizing about every 2 weeks.

Dusty miller *(Senecio cineraria)* is one of the most widely planted perennial senecios. It's hardy to about 0°F/−18°C. Plants grow to 2–2½-foot mounds of wooly white leaves, each leaf long and tongue shaped, but cut into many blunt-tipped lobes. Yellow flower heads come in clusters sporadically during the year.

Grow it in full sun, average soil. Give moderate watering and pinch back plant occasionally.

Shasta daisy. See **Chrysanthemum**.

Shell flower. See **Moluccella**.

Shirley poppy. See **Papaver**.

Snapdragon. See **Antirrhinum**.

Sneezeweed. See **Helenium**.

Snow-in-summer. See **Cerastium**.

Snow-on-the-mountain. See **Euphorbia**.

Speedwell. See **Veronica**.

Spider flower. See **Cleome**.

Spurge. See **Euphorbia**.

Stachys byzantina

Lamb's ears
Perennial, hardy to −35°F/−37°C

This familiar, useful ground cover and edging plant is valued for its 6-inch elliptical leaves that are thick, gray, and covered with white woolly hairs. Plants spread and sprawl, thoroughly covering the ground and mounding up to about 1 foot. Short spikes of tiny purplish red flowers appear atop 12–18-inch stems in summer, but they're not particularly showy. Plants sold as *S. lanata* and *S. olympica* are included in this species.

Not fussy about soil, lamb's ears need full sun or light shade, good drainage, moderate watering.

Statice. See **Limonium**.

Stock. See **Matthiola**.

Stokes aster. See **Stokesia**.

Stokesia laevis

Stokes aster
Perennial, hardy to −20°F/−29°C

Clumps of long, narrowly elliptical leaves support 1½-foot stems that

Stokesia

bear clusters of 3–4-inch blossoms. The flowers resemble asters or large cornflowers. The basic color is blue, and the variety usually sold is 'Blue Danube'; a cool-white selection is 'Silver Moon.' These are trouble-free plants for foreground color in summer through early autumn.

Set out plants in full sun, in average but well-drained soil, and give moderate to regular watering. In time clumps will become crowded and need dividing; do this in early spring.

Stonecrop. See **Sedum.**

Strawflower. See **Helichrysum.**

Summer chrysanthemum.
  See **Chrysanthemum.**

Summer forget-me-not. See **Anchusa.**

Summer phlox. See **Phlox.**

Sundrop. See **Oenothera.**

Sunflower. See **Helianthus.**

Swan River daisy. See **Brachycome.**

Sweet alyssum. See **Lobularia.**

Sweet pea. See **Lathyrus.**

Sweet sultan. See **Centaurea.**

Sweet violet. See **Viola.**

Sweet William. See **Dianthus.**

T

Tagetes

Marigold
Annual
Pictured on pages 19, 30, 36, 38

Marigolds offer almost too wide a selection of size and color, at least for indecisive gardeners. Plants range in height from 6–36 inches or more. Blossoms vary from ¾-inch petites to 5-inch giants, and may be single or double. Colors include shades of maroon, dark red, orange, yellow, and mixtures of these, and white. Kinds include African (*Tagetes erecta*), French (*Tagetes patula*), and signet (*Tagetes tenuifolia*), and their numerous strains and varieties. No wonder it's difficult to make a choice!

Marigolds are worth choosing, though. They're sturdy, long-blooming, easy-to-grow plants that have many uses: background plantings, edgings, containers, mixed plantings, and cut flowers.

Marigolds grow quickly from seeds. Sow them directly in the garden in spring when the soil is warm, or set out plants from a nursery for a faster start. Give them good, well-drained soil, full sun, ample water. Once blooming starts, remove faded blossoms to insure a new supply.

Thalictrum

Meadow rue
Perennial, hardy to −20°F/−29°C; not suited to Gulf coast and Florida

Meadow rue shows many similarities to its cousin, columbine: fernlike, graceful foliage that's often blue green in tone, and a preference for woodland-edge situations. However, meadow rue is generally much larger than columbine. Leafy flower stems rise 2–6 feet high, depending upon the species. Flower clusters are much branched and open, bearing many small 4-part blooms each with a prominent cluster of stamens. Flower colors include purple, lavender, rosy lilac, violet, white, and yellow.

Meadow rue thrives in moist but well-drained soil with plenty of organic matter. Woodland conditions—dappled sunlight or light shade—are best. Plants may be divided for increase in spring, but may also remain undisturbed for years.

Tithonia

Mexican sunflower
Annual

Tall tithonia, boasting vivid red orange flowers, reaches its zenith of striking beauty in late summer where the weather is hot and dry. A desert native, the robust, coarse-leafed plants grow 3–6 feet high and spread to an equal width. The flowers are 3–4 inches wide and good for cutting. Handle cut flowers delicately though; stalks are hollow and brittle.

Plant seeds in warm soil outdoors; later thin seedlings to 4 feet apart so they'll have room to spread. In cold-winter areas, plant seeds indoors in pots during early spring. By the time frost danger is past, plants will be ready to set out for August bloom. Tithonia takes plenty of sun and only light watering.

Trillium

Wake robin
Perennial, hardiness varies

The trilliums are woodland-dwelling harbingers of spring. Their name stems from the fact that some plant parts are in threes: 3 broadly oval leaves top a fairly short stem, and a 3-petaled blossom is carried on or just above the leaves. Clumps of foliage are handsome; the flowers of some are showy and elegant. Colors include white, yellow, green, pink, and purple. All need some winter chilling.

Plant trilliums in dappled sunlight to shade, in good soil heavily enriched with organic matter. The fleshy rhizomes should go about 2 inches deep. Give plants regular watering; never let them go dry. Trilliums increase slowly, forming increasingly attractive clumps; there's no need to dig and divide them.

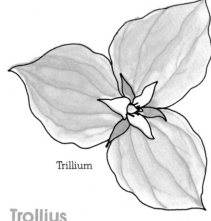

Trillium

Trollius

Globeflower
Perennial, hardy to −35°F/−35°C; not suited to desert regions, Gulf coast, and Florida

Globeflowers offer brilliant blossoms and good-looking, well-behaved plants. From clumps of finely cut, rather celerylike leaves, rise 2 to 2½-foot-tall stems that terminate in yellow to orange, roundly cupped blossoms. Flowering is late spring to late summer, depending on the variety. Blooming may be prolonged if you remove spent flowers.

Moisture is key to globeflower success. Give them a well-drained soil enriched with plenty of organic matter, and water them regularly. They will grow around pools and along streams as long as soil is not saturated. They prefer filtered sun to light shade. In time, when clumps decline in vigor or thin out at the centers, plants should be dug, divided, and reset. Late summer to early autumn is the best time.

Tropaeolum majus

Nasturtium
Annual. Perennial where frosts are light
Pictured on page 41

Nasturtiums are so easy to grow that they smile rewards on beginning gardeners as young as age five. These colorful flowers have yet another delightful virtue — they're edible, with a peppery, watercress flavor that puts zest into salads and soups.

Single or double-petaled blossoms, about 2 inches across, come in a full palette of warm colors and bicolors — from root-beer brown and maroon through reds, oranges, and yellows to pure cream.

Nasturtiums trail and climb as high as 6 feet, or they grow as smaller bushes, 8–15 inches high. Their seeds, as large as peas, need only a poke into the ground. Plant seeds in a permanent location when the weather is warm, since nasturtiums do not transplant well. Most abundant bloom is in fairly poor soil and full sun.

V

Verbascum

Mullein
Biennial. Perennial, hardy to −30°F/−34°C
Pictured on page 34

From a rosette of foliage rises a spire closely set with nearly flat, circular, rather ruffled flowers about 1 inch across. Some have single flower spikes, others have branched spikes.

Biennial types form their foliage in one year, send up flowering spikes the following summer, set much seed, and die.

Different kinds range from 2–5 feet tall and have white or yellow flowers. Several perennial species and hybrids are available. They grow from 3–5 feet tall and have white, yellow, pink, purple, or red flowers.

All the mulleins are tough and undemanding. Give them well-drained, but not too rich soil and moderate water. Cut off spent flower spikes to prevent seeds from forming. Many verbascums self-sow prolifically, and tap-rooted seedlings are a nuisance to dig out.

Verbena

Perennial; many grown as annuals
Pictured on pages 21, 28, 59

Verbenas have many admirable qualities — they're long-blooming, low-growing, drought-resistant plants with a wide range of colors. Besides that, most of them grow rapidly from seeds and spread wide in a single season. That makes them good candidates for small-scale ground covers, especially in hot, dry areas.

Garden verbena (*Verbena hybrida*), a short-lived perennial where winters are mild, is usually grown as an annual. Plants grow 6–12 inches high, and spread 1½–3 feet. Foliage is bright green or gray green; flowers, in clusters, are red, pink, white, blue, purple, and combinations. Some kinds are scented; some make good container plants.

Sow seeds or set out plants in the garden in full sun when the soil has warmed in spring. Once plants are established, water them deeply and not too often.

Verbena peruviana, another perennial that's grown as an annual, spreads fast, making a very low mat. Flowers are red, white, pink, or purple. Set out plants and give them the same conditions and care as for garden verbena.

Verbena rigida, a perennial that's hardy to 10°F/−12°C, has naturalized in parts of the South. Plants grow 10–20 inches tall, bear lilac to purple blue flowers in clusters on tall stiff stems. Set out plants in spring, and treat like other verbenas. They grow fast from seeds, so they can be used as annuals.

Verbena canadensis, native to the United States, is hardy to 0°F/−18°C. Selected varieties are low growing. Colors include rose purple, pink, white. Treat like other verbenas. It will also grow as an annual.

Veronica

Speedwell
Perennial, hardy to −30°F/−34°C
Pictured on page 35

Taller *Veronica* species and hybrids are best known for their blue shades in the summer garden. Individual flowers are tiny, but most often come in closely-packed, tapering spikes above shrubby clumps of narrow, pointed leaves. Those with flower stems reaching to 2 feet are *V. grandis holophylla*, *V. incana*, *V. longifolia subsessilis*, and *V. spicata*. The first has dark glossy leaves and spikes of deep blue blossoms. *V. incana* is more sprawling; its bright blue flowers contrast with grayish leaves and stems. *V. longifolia subsessilis* is upright and full-foliaged, also dark blue. *V. spicata* is similar but less robust and with shorter flower spikes. The hybrids tend to be bushy and upright, in a variety of colors and heights. 'Barcarole' and 'Minuet' are pink 1–1½ feet tall with grayish green foliage; 'Icicle' is a 1½-foot white. In blue tones are foot-high 'Crater Lake Blue', dark blue 'Blue Charm' and 'Blue Peter' (both about 1½ feet tall), and vivid blue violet 'Sarabande', also about 1½ feet.

Average good garden soil, well drained, will suit the veronicas. Give them full sun or filtered sunlight and regular watering. When clumps

Veronica

show signs of declining vigor, dig and divide them in early spring or early autumn.

Viola

Viola, Pansy, Violet
Perennial, hardiness varies; some grown as annuals
Pictured on pages 20, 38, 39, 61

What would springtime be without the cheery faces of pansies, violas, and violets? From early spring until summer's heat arrives, they brighten the shady corners of gardens and woodlands. With low-growing habits, and a wide range of colors, they are excellent for growing in masses, combinations, or containers.

Violas (*Viola cornuta*) grow in little clumps 6–8 inches high. Flowers are 1½ inches wide, mostly in solid colors of yellow, apricot, ruby red, blue, purple, and white.

Where winters are mild, sow seeds in late summer; set out plants in autumn for winter and spring bloom. In cold-winter areas, either sow seeds in September, keep in cold frame over winter, and set plants out in early spring; or sow seeds indoors in January or February and set plants out in early spring for spring to summer flowers. Grow in rich, cool, moist soil in a partly shady location. Pinch off faded blossoms to prolong blooming.

Pansies (*Viola wittrockiana*) grow in clumps 6–8 inches high. Flowers can get 2–4 inches wide in blue, purple, yellow, apricot, orange, mahogany red, white, and bicolors. Petals usually have stripes or dark blotches. Recent hybrids bloom more freely and are more heat tolerant. They have the same culture requirements as violas.

Johnny-jump-up (*Viola tricolor*) grows in tufts, either as an annual or a short-lived perennial. Plants are 6–12 inches tall; flowers are like small pansies, usually purple and yellow. They, too, have the same culture requirements as violas.

Violets, many with delicious fragrance, are the truly perennial violas. You can use them in woodland gardens; the less aggressive kinds do well in shady borders. They also make good small-scale ground covers. Some violets form compact clumps, others spread by sending out runners that root at joints. Some kinds self-sow. All have roundish

heart-shaped leaves at the ends of long leaf stalks.

Sweet violet (*Viola odorata*), hardy to −10°F/−24°C, is the best known for fragrance. Named varieties are available in white, pink, and purple and violet shades. Plant height varies from 2–10 inches. Plants spread by runners. Fragrant Parma violets (*V. alba*) are similar, but with double flowers and less hardiness (to 0°F/ −18°C).

Hardy to 20°F/−7°C is Australian violet (*V. hederacea*); the 4-inch-high plants spread slowly, bearing white, or blue and white blossoms. Varieties of *V. cucullata*, hardy to −30°F/ −34°C, may have flowers of blue or white, with reddish centers or white, blue, and yellow combined; plants are clump-forming. Confederate violet (*V. sororia*, sometimes sold as *V. priceana*), has larger leaves and larger, flatter flowers than the other species; color is white, veined dark blue or gray blue.

Where summers are cool, violets will perform well in sun; but where summers are hotter, violets need shade. Prepare soil with plenty of organic matter, and water plants regularly.

Violet. See **Viola**

Viscaria. See **Lychnis**

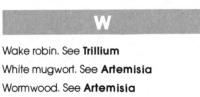

Wake robin. See **Trillium**

White mugwort. See **Artemisia**

Wormwood. See **Artemisia**

Yarrow. See **Achillea**

Z

Zantedeschia

Calla
Perennial, hardy to 10°F/−12°C
Pictured on page 53

Sculptural, elegant callas have long, celerylike leaf stalks that end in glossy, elongated, arrow-shaped leaves. Rising above the foliage are flowering stalks each bearing what

appears to be a cornucopia-shaped flower (actually, a bract surrounding a central spike that contains minute flowers).

The most common calla is *Z. aethiopica*: 3 feet tall with 8-inch white bracts in spring and early summer and 18-inch leaves. Other callas have yellow, pink, or purple-throated white bracts. Plants vary in height from 1–2 feet and some have white-spotted leaves. Hybrid callas encompass various pastel shades including tawny, buff, and lavender to purple tones.

Common calla (*Z. aethiopica*) grows well with regular watering, but flourishes with much more. Set rhizomes about 4 inches deep. Plant is evergreen where winters are mild, deciduous in colder regions.

All other callas are deciduous. They should be planted about 2 inches deep in well-drained soil and watered regularly. In colder regions, if soil is poorly drained during winter, dig and store them over winter as for canna (see page 70). Treat them this way, too, in regions where winters are ordinarily too cold to survive.

Zinnia

Annual
Pictured on pages 35, 38, 54

Flamboyant flamenco dancers of the summer flower garden, zinnias are anything but boring. They come in a great diversity of sizes and colors (blue is the only tint missing from the zinnia palette). Their bright coiffures (flowers), ranging from neat-as-a-pin to shaggy, span from 1–7 inches across. Plants come as short as 6 inches and as lofty as 3 feet. Use small ones to edge borders, tall ones for background plantings. They're superb cutting flowers.

Whatever their shape and size and color, zinnias have one requirement: heat. They'll just sit still if the weather's cool. They're at their best in the hot, lazy days of late summer and early autumn.

In spring or early summer, sow seeds in full sun and a warm location, preferably where there's good air circulation (to prevent mildew). Give enough water to keep growth steady, but don't overwater; and (to prevent mildew) don't splash the leaves (soak the soil instead). Give fertilizer regularly.

Index